THE WIS ROAD GUIDE TO GANGSTER HOT SPOTS

BY: CHAD LEWIS

THE WISCONSIN ROAD GUIDE TO GANGSTER HOT SPOTS

The Wisconsin Road Guide to Gangster Hot Spots
Copyright 2010
ISBN: 978-0-9824314-1-2
On The Road Publications
www.ontheroadpublications.com

Author: Chad Lewis

Acknowledgments

I would like to thank Nisa Giaquinto, Noah Voss, Sarah Szymanski, and Loren Evenrud, for assisting me with the research and production of the book.

I would also like to thank the numerous historical societies, librarians, and fellow researchers who provided extensive research for this book. I would like to give a special thanks to those who took the time and effort to share their memories with me about the crimes that impacted their families and communities.

DEDICATION

This book is dedicated to all of my Lewis relatives who have kept alive the tradition of Wisconsin being the home of interesting characters.

The Wisconsin Road Guide to Gangster Hot Spots

Table of Contents

The Wisconsin Road Guide to Gangster Hot Spots

Table of Contents

The Wisconsin Road Guide to Gangster Hot Spots

Table of Contents

FOREWORD

The Wisconsin Road Guide to Gangster Hot Spots is an engaging narrative that traces the steps of a number of notorious 1930's Chicago gangsters in Northern Wisconsin. The "rough and tumble" existing tourist and resort industry provided perfect cover for the likes of Baby Face Nelson, Tommy Carroll, John Dillinger, and Al Capone. The region was sprinkled with a cast of local "jack pine" characters that profited from popular brothels and illegal liquor sales. Law enforcement interference was rare.

Chad Lewis tracks gangster legends and folklore down the back roads as well as in small communities such as Arlington, Couderay, Lac du Flambeau, Minocqua, Winter, and Woodruff. He has a keen eye for locating the modern day locations for the Arlington Inn, Baker Lake Lodge ("Gentleman" Joe Saltis), Capone's Northwoods Hideout, Dillman's Bay Resort, and the infamous Ma Bailey's Bordello.

Like the street gangs of today, the Chicago gangsters imported a "lawless lifestyle" to the Wisconsin north woods that often blurred the distinction between folk hero and common criminal. It is ironic that vehicles bearing Illinois license plates still flood the Northern Highland resort region of Wisconsin during the warm months of summer.

Loren A. Evenrud, Ph.D.
Adjunct Professor
Department of Criminal Justice
Concordia University

I

Introduction

The state of Wisconsin is one amazingly interesting place. Overlooked in the public's perception of crazed Packers fans, cheese, beer, and dairy farmers rests Wisconsin's gangster past. I came across this unique history by sheer happenstance. I was traveling the state while doing research for the *Wisconsin Road Guide to Haunted Locations* when I popped a tire in the middle of the Northwoods. Looking for a safe place to make the repair, I pulled over next to the entrance of a place called Little Bohemia. The old place looked like had been trapped in time since the early 1900s. Having worked up a thirst from the tire repair, I decided to venture inside to grab a pop and find out what this unique looking place was all about. Needless to say from the moment I entered the building, I was floored by its history. Way in the back of the lodge was a glass case showcasing items left behind by gangsters who fled the place in a 1934 shootout with authorities. Now I was born and raised in Wisconsin, and had traveled every last inch of the state, and yet somehow all mention of gangsters had completely escaped me. Determined to learn all I could about Wisconsin's gangsters, I embarked on a state-wide journey to find the places where the gangsters impacted Wisconsin. Let me say that I had no idea how prevalent gangsters once were in Wisconsin, a fact you will soon discover for yourself.

The research aspect for this book was truly an adventure. I explored the places where gangsters robbed banks, shot it out with the law, took people "for a ride," and danced the night away. Along the way I found myself stuck in a snow bank outside of Capone's Hideout, searching a fireplace for a buried gangster, breaking up a serious game of Euchre, and spending days tracking down an eyewitness who actually saw Baby Face Nelson crash his car. By the end of my journey I had explored the entire state in search of the men and women who, for good or bad, changed the history of Wisconsin. But I did not write this book simply for you to read and then forget, I wrote it to be a guide for you to get out and enjoy these sites for yourself. Grab your zoot suit and Tommy Guns, well… maybe leave your guns at home, and follow in the footsteps of some of the most dangerous men in America. Go along as they hid out from the police, terrorized towns, robbed banks, and "disposed" of anyone who got in their way. Let this book be your guide as you transport yourself back to the roaring 1920s and 30s. To ensure that you get the maxim amount of pleasure from your trip take some advice from the gangsters themselves who always stuck to the back roads, avoided the big hotels, always sat with their back to the wall, and had plenty of aliases. If you follow these simple steps, you might just find yourself agreeing that Wisconsin is truly one amazingly interesting place.

Keep an eye out,
Chad Lewis

Robbers
Strike Bank

Shoot-Out

Wanted

ROGUES
GALLERY

REWARD

Murder!

Kidnapping

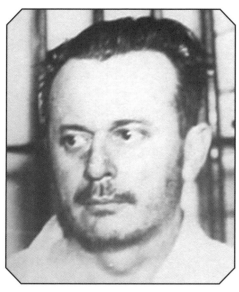

Arthur "Doc" Barker- Doc was born in Missouri in 1899. From an early age Barker was in and out of prison and was best known for teaming up with his brother Fred Barker, and fellow gangster Alvin "Creepy" Karpis. Doc was eventually sentenced to Alcatraz where he was killed while attempting to escape.

Fred Barker- Was described by many as a cold-blooded killer. Barker formed the Barker-Karpis gang with his brother Doc Barker, and Alvin Karpis. Fred met his end when he and his mother were shot to death during a 1935 raid on their Florida rental cabin.

V

Ma Barker- Ma Barker was born Arizona Donnie Clark in Missouri. She was portrayed as the outlaw mother of the Barker boys. After being killed in a shootout in Florida, the FBI fabricated the legend of the woman, who it was said could not plan breakfast, much less a bank robbery. Ma Barker was killed in 1935 alongside her son Fred in a shootout at their Florida rental cabin.

Al Capone – Capone was born in Brooklyn and as a teenager found himself wrapped up in the criminal element. Circumstances forced Capone to Chicago where he began his rise to the top of the bootlegging business. Best known as being the man behind the St. Valentine's Day Massacre, Capone was convicted of tax evasion in 1931 and sent to Alcatraz Prison. In 1939, with his health failing, Capone was paroled and moved to his home in Florida. In 1947, Capone suffered a stroke and passed away.

Ralph Capone- Ralph Capone was Al's big brother and spent many years working the underworld for his famous brother. Ralph was an avid outdoorsman and built his hunting lodge in Mercer, Wisconsin, where he eventually settled. Deemed a wonderful citizen by those who knew him, Ralph died in Wisconsin in 1974.

Tommy Carroll- Born in Montana, Carroll was a Chicago area bank robber who worked closely with John Dillinger, Baby Face Nelson, and Homer Van Meter. Carroll was killed by two detectives in Waterloo, Iowa in 1934.

John Paul Chase- Chase lived a mostly straight life in California until he accepted a job as an armed guard for a truck smuggling illegal liquor. Chase's co-worker on the job was George "Baby Face" Nelson. While working together the two men became fast friends. Chase spent time with Nelson in Lake Geneva. In 1934, after the death of Baby Face, Chase was eventually arrested and sentenced to Alcatraz Prison. Over the years, Chase was transferred to several prisons until his final release in 1966. In 1973, Chase succumbed to cancer and died in California.

Russell Clark- Clark escaped from the Indiana State Prison and began his career with John Dillinger. Clark was the driver in the Racine bank robbery. Eventually Clark was apprehended in Tucson and spent 34 years in prison before being released just before his death in 1968.

Marie "Mickey" Conforti- Conforti was the girlfriend of Dillinger pal, Homer Van Meter. Conforti was captured by the Feds after the shootout at Little Bohemia. After Van Meter was gunned down in St. Paul, Conforti turned herself in to the FBI. Even though she cooperated with the authorities, Conforti was convicted of harboring a fugitive (Van Meter) and served one year and one day in prison.

Jean Delaney- Delaney was an attractive young blond, who while separated from her husband, was seeing Dillinger gang member Tommy Carroll. In 1934, Delaney was captured after the shootout at Little Bohemia. Delaney also spent some time in with Carroll in Lake Geneva, WI. After witnessing Tommy Carroll get gunned down in Iowa,

Delaney was sentenced to the Alderson Industrial Institution in West Virginia, where she served one year and one day. After prison Delaney lived a normal and quiet life.

John Dillinger- Born in Indiana in 1903, John Dillinger went on to become the nation's most famous bank robber during the 1930s. Dillinger was considered Public Enemy #1 when he was gunned down outside Chicago's Biograph Theater in 1934.

Arthur Dunlop- Dunlop was best known for dating Ma Barker. A real talker when he drank, Dunlop was "taken for a ride" and killed by the Barker-Karpis gang in 1932. His naked body was discovered near a lake in Oakland, Wisconsin.

Helen Gillis- Helen Wawrzyniak (Gillis) was best known as the loving wife of Lester "Baby Face Nelson" Gillis. Together the couple had two children. Those who spotted the couple together recalled that they were nearly inseparable. Helen's only crime was that she was completely in love with her outlaw husband. Helen was captured after the shootout at Little Bohemia. After the death of Baby Face in 1934, Helen lived a long and quiet life before passing in 1987. Helen was buried next to her husband at St. Joseph's Cemetery in River Grove, IL.

Alvin "Old Creepy" Karpis- Karpis, who was born Alvin Karpowicz, was best known for joining forces with the Barker gang. Karpis was considered one of the smartest gangsters of his time. Karpis was finally captured in 1936, and sent to Alcatraz Prison where he spent more time than any other inmate before being paroled in 1969. Karpis died in 1979 from a pill overdose.

John Hamilton- A.K.A.- Red, Three Finger Jack. – Hamilton met John Dillinger while the two of them were in prison together. After prison Hamilton went on a crime spree with Dillinger and was killed in Hastings, MN., during a car chase with authorities

Tommy Holden- Holden was part of the infamous Holden-Keating gang that held up a U.S. Mail truck in Illinois. Holden was sent to the Leavenworth Federal Penitentiary where he and Francis Keating would escape in 1930. After a series of robberies including the Kraft State Bank in Menomonie, WI., Holden was once again captured and sent to Alcatraz Prison.

Holden was paroled in 1947. Two years later in 1949, Holden, in a drunken stupor killed his wife and two of her brothers. In 1951, Holden was finally captured and sent back to prison where he died in 1953.

Francis Keating- Keating was the other important member of the Holden-Keating gang. After he and Tommy Holden robbed the U.S Mail truck he was sent to prison. Escaping in 1930, Keating headed right back into the gangster lifestyle and helped rob the Kraft State Bank in Wisconsin, along with many other crimes. Keating was arrested on a golf course and sent off to Alcatraz Prison. It is believed that unlike most of his colleagues, when Keating was paroled from Alcatraz he lived his life on the straight and narrow, and died peacefully in the Twin Cities.

Charles Makley - Makley was born in Ohio and started his outlaw life from an early age. In and out of jail, Makley ended up meeting John Dillinger while serving time in Indiana. Makley was one of ten inmates that were busted out of prison with the aid of Dillinger. Part of the group that robbed the Racine Bank, Makley was captured in Tuscan and sent back to prison. In 1934, Makley was killed during a botched prison escape with his colleague Harry Pierpont.

George "Bugs" Moran- Moran, a native of Minnesota, was a powerful bootlegger operating in Chicago. Involved in numerous wars with Capone and other rival gangs, Moran seemed to always escape death, most notably when he barely avoided getting killed at the St. Valentine's Day Massacre. Many researchers credit Moran with originating the drive-by shooting. In 1957, Moran died of lung cancer inside the Leavenworth Federal Penitentiary. It is believed that when Moran died he was virtually destitute.

George "Baby Face" Nelson- Real Name Lester Gillis. Baby Face was born in Chicago in 1908, and was on the wrong side of the law from an early age. Mostly considered a hotheaded killer, Nelson was perhaps the best connected gangster in the Midwest. Often Nelson was the one to secure safe houses, weapons, cars, and unsavory business associates for his colleagues. During his legacy of crime and

murder, Nelson was married with two children, and was described as a devoted husband. In 1934, Nelson died in a shoot out with police just outside of Chicago.

Harry Pierpont-Pierpont was born in Indiana in 1902. Pierpont was considered one of Dillinger's main mentors. In 1933, Dillinger showed his loyalty to Pierpont by helping to break him out of prison. Pierpont was involved with the Racine bank robbery. Pierpont was captured in Tuscan and sent back to prison, where he was riddled with bullets while trying to escape with Charles Makley. Surviving the escape attempt, Pierpont was put to death in the electric chair in 1934.

Gentleman Joe Saltis- Saltis was a beer baron from Chicago who moved to the Northwoods of Wisconsin to escape the deadly gang wars. Saltis made a fortune during Prohibition and at one point the majority of people in town worked at his WI lodge. Saltis avoided any serious prison time and eventually faded away from the criminal world. In 1947, Saltis died penniless in Illinois.

Homer Van Meter- Van Meter was an associate of both Baby Face Nelson and John Dillinger, who he met while serving time in prison. Newspapers of the 1930s claimed that Van Meter was Dillinger's Lieutenant. Van Meter was shot to death in an alley in St. Paul.

MENOMONIE, WI

BLOODY ROBBERY
OF THE KRAFT STATE BANK

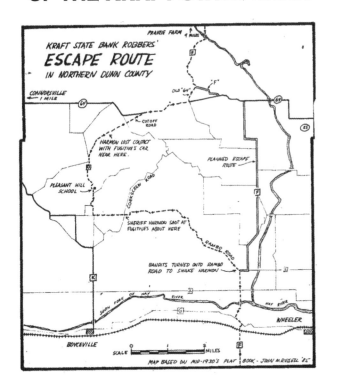

Bloody Robbery of the Kraft State Bank

Location:

M&I Bank Parking Lot

500 Main Street East

Menomonie, WI 54751

Directions:

The former Kraft State Bank was located in downtown
Menomonie on Highway 12. The bank was positioned in
the spot where the M&I Bank parking lot is today.

Gangster Lore:

During the Depression era, news reports concerning bank
robberies were a common everyday occurrence. For the
most part these bank robberies usually went relatively
smooth, and the only thing that got hurt was the bank's

wallet. To help protect themselves from any police officers or pubic heroes shooting at them, the robbers regularly used bank employees as human shields. However, if the use of force became necessary, the outlaws certainly did not hesitate in using it to the fullest. Often the authorities quickly discovered that not only were they terribly out-gunned, but they were also dealing with the type of people that felt innocent lives mattered little when pitted against their own survival. Even with all the precautions taken to ensure the safety of the citizens, small gun battles regularly erupted during bank heists. Most of the time the surrounding buildings took the majority of the gun damage while human casualties remained low. Unfortunately, this was not the case when the gangsters turned the Kraft State Bank robbery into one of Wisconsin's bloodiest.

History:
1914 – The Kraft State Bank was founded by Phillip Kraft and his sons John, William, and Samuel.

1931 – Four armed bandits robbed the Kraft State Bank.

1970s-early 80s – The Kraft State Bank building was torn down.

Currently – The old bank building location is a parking lot.

Investigation:
No one seemed to notice the large black Lincoln as it slowly strolled along Main Street. It was just after 9am

on October 20, 1931, as the automobile pulled over and parked next to Frank Hintzman's Funeral Parlor. With the bloodshed that was about to occur, the irony of their parking choice was unmistakable. Frank Webber, who was positioned behind the wheel, would serve as the getaway driver. Webber left the engine running while Francis Keating, Tommy Holden, and Charles Preston Harmon calmly hopped out of the car and hurriedly headed down towards the Kraft State Bank. These dangerous men were all lifelong criminals, and Holden and Keating were wanted fugitives who had recently escaped from Leavenworth Prison. The men knew that the bank had just opened for the day, a fact that the gangsters hoped would limit the number of customers inside. The gangsters had spent days casing the place, vigilantly watching the bank in order to learn its schedule and routine. Now as they approached the bank's main entrance, all of their planning was about to pay off in the form of increased riches. Gangsters called Menomonie the "crooked bridge town", due to the hazards the slow moving and winding turns of the town's bridges presented them. Many of the robbers of the day felt like the risks of robbing a bank in Menomonie far outweighed the benefits. Bank robbing was a dangerous profession, a fact that all of the gangsters knew too well. Yet even with this understanding, the men walking into the Kraft State Bank had no idea that for some of them this heist would be their last.

The men quickly entered the bank and forced the ten employees and four customers to lie down on the ground. Immediately the outlaws started scoping all of the cash from the tellers' cages. Once all of the small money was secured, the men grabbed bank cashier William S. Kraft and demanded to know where the rest of the money was. Whether or not he actually knew where the money was Kraft panicked and foolishly told them that the bank had no additional funds, which of course was not the answer the men were looking for. The *Sheboygan Press* wrote that "without warning, one of the desperadoes fired a .45 caliber revolver from close range." The *Waterloo Daily Courier* expanded on the story claiming, "Kraft was shot in the side as he lay on the floor. The leader of the raiders refused to accept his word that they had all the cash, cursed and threatened him with death and then fired point blank. Physicians believed Kraft's lung may have been punctured." The *Waterloo Daily Courier* wrote, "Vernon Townsend, bank guard, commanded a view of the interior from a bullet proof cage on a balcony was told he should press an alarm button and then go to the roof and fire at the bandits' car." Townsend followed his instructions and set off the alarm before sneaking out the back door and heading to the roof.

The sounding of the alarm had alerted the waiting Webber that something had gone terribly wrong. Webber moved slowly to the front of Kern's Lakeside Café, where he left the car running in the middle of the street. Webber quickly got out and opened up both doors on the left side for his partners and started waving his Tommy Gun back and forth across the street to dissuade anyone from aiding the bank. Webber wasn't the only one to hear the alarm, and soon local residents grabbed their guns and joined the fight. The robbers knew that with a gathering posse they would need some hostages to protect them and decided to grab James Kraft and Mrs. A.W. Schafer. Bank guard Townsend was already propped up on the roof, but the getaway car was parked in such a way that he could only fire at the rear. Even with his limited angle Townsend believed that one of his shots had punctured the gas tank. A minute later the gangsters were busting out of the front door and heading for their car. Kraft was shoved into the car, while seeing all of the excitement was just too much for Mrs. A.W. Schafer, who froze with fear and dropped to the ground. Her frightened response likely saved her life because the gangsters were more concerned with their safety than hers, and simply left Schafer behind as they jumped into the getaway car and tore off.

While the bandits were attempting to escape local restaurant owner Winfield Kern was itching to join the fight. In fact, Kern's enthusiasm overwhelmed his common sense when he fired through his own store window for a chance to hit the fleeing gangsters. Another store clerk, Ed Grutt, also tried his hand at being a vigilante and fired on the robbers as well. For their part, the gangsters blasted back at the town when Webber released a volley of bullets. During the raging gunfight, Webber was struck in the eye by one of the whizzing bullets. The *Ogden Standard-Examiner* reported, "Ed Krinkig (Grutt), a witness to the holdup claimed he heard one of the bandits cry out when he fired his rifle at the back of the car."

In an odd scenario Kraft was forced to drive the getaway car and was as ordered to steer east down Highway 12. To make matters worse another gangster, Charles

Preston Harmon, was also wounded by the onslaught of gunfire. Witnesses reported the gangsters turned onto County Trunk B as they looked to drive toward safety. Along the way the men utilized their low-tech escape plan and scattered the roads with roofing tacks to help disrupt any police chase. During the drive Webber succumbed to his gunshot wound and passed away in the car. Needless to say the robbery did not go off according to plan, and now the gangsters were looking for revenge. Unfortunately, that revenge would be taken out on their hostage as the police believed it was after Webber's death that the men put a bullet into the back of Kraft's head. The *Montana Butte Standard* wrote that officers "were satisfied Kraft was not shot by pursuers. The manner in which he was shot and the fact that the car did not reduce speed as it left the city indicate he was slain later." Adding more evidence to this claim was the statement printed in the *Ironwood Daily Globe* from Coroner Carl Olsen who said, "Kraft's wounds were caused by a type of bullet the pursuers did not have." The dead bodies of both Webber and Kraft were unceremoniously dumped on the side of the road near a farm owned by the Ranney family. Knowing that the authorities would soon be on their trail, the gangsters sped off toward several gas cans that had previously been strategically placed along the road.

A very bad day was about to get worse for the gangsters as Harmon continued to wail in pain caused by the gunshot wounds to his neck and knee. The next day it became apparent to the men that Harmon would die without receiving medical attention. Harmon's bloody body was already attracting unwanted attention, and the gangsters could not take the chance of him dying, so when the outlaws passed an abandoned farm near Shell Lake, they pulled over and laid Harmon down on the ground. Harmon was still alive at the time he was dropped off, and his colleagues placed about $1,000 in stolen securities with him that would serve to get him through if he somehow survived— which he did not. A passing 14-year-old girl stumbled upon Harmon who was frantically grabbing at the dirt as he writhed in pain. The young girl notified the authorities and upon arrival they located Harmon's dead body. During their investigation of the body they found that he was still wearing his bullet proof vest, and it was soon discovered that one of the bullets had penetrated his vest causing his death. Somewhere along the line the remaining gangsters discarded their old, bloody, bullet-ridden car and replaced it with something clean. The *Evening Huronite* wrote that "the trail of the bandits was followed several miles and their car, blood spattered, was later found. Officers believe the trio continued flight in another machine."

Back in Menomonie, the Sheriff had aborted his chase of the gangsters and returned to town to organize the manhunt. To help with his pursuit, the sheriff hastily deputized 32 local men who were all willing to risk their lives in the search for the fugitives. Meanwhile, Holden and Keating continued on easily and escaped into the back roads of Wisconsin. Their freedom would not last forever, however, as nearly eight months later Holden and Keating were arrested in Kansas City, Missouri. The fugitives were sent back to Leavenworth Prison. The amount of money taken from the bank was first reported to be around $7,000. However, later accounts report the loss of cash and securities to be over $100,000.

Tommy Gun Adventures:

The robbery of 1931 comes alive with a short trip over to the Dunn County Historical Society headquarters at 1820 Wakanda Street in Menomonie, (715) 232-8685. Here you will find an in-depth interactive display of the robbery including several pieces of memorabilia.

Egg Harbor, WI

The Historic Shipwrecked Pub

The Historic Shipwrecked Pub

Location:
Shipwrecked Brew Pub
7791 State Highway 42
Egg Harbor, WI 54209
(920) 868-2767
www.shipwreckedmicrobrew.com

Directions:
The brew pub is located right on Highway 42 in Egg Harbor.

Gangster Lore:
Outside of bank robbing, murdering, bootlegging, kidnapping, prostitution, gambling, bribing, and extortion, most of the gangsters of the early days were very much like us. As facetious as that sounds, it is actually stated with some sincerity. Overall, the gangsters desired mostly the same things in life that we "normal" people do. So when it came to taking vacations, it only seemed natural that they, like so many of us today, would head up to the lovely tourist destination of Door County.

History:

Late 1800s – The tavern and inn was established to cater to the influx of lumbermen, sailors, and passing stagecoach travelers. This one-stop-shop provided food, lodging, and spirits.

1920s – Gangsters flocked to Door County while on vacation. The old inn provided the perfect place to stop in and enjoy an illegal beverage or two.

1930s-1960s – The restaurant/inn was operated as Murphy Moore's.

1996 – Robert and Noreen Pollman purchased the business, which at the time was known as the Harbor Point.

1997 – The new owners opened Shipwrecked Restaurant, Brewery & Inn.

Currently – The brew pub and inn is open to the public.

Investigation:

In the early days of Door County the remote area mostly relied on the lumber trade for its survival. With the harbor so close, the area was inundated with working sailors and lumbermen seeking out a place where they could unwind from the backbreaking work day. They needed someplace that offered both a hearty meal and plenty of fine spirits to wash away any memory of the exhausting labor. Luckily for them the tavern and inn was exactly the type of place they were after, and the old inn's close proximity to the harbor provided the men with the ideal socializing space.

During the 1920s, Door County became a popular hot spot for vacationing gangsters. Underworld characters traveled to the shore to escape both the literal and figurative heat that plagued them down south. Residents of the area got used to seeing the gangsters driving through town in luxury automobiles. In a time of frugality before the Depression, it didn't take a keen eye to spot the gangsters walking around in their tailor-made suits, especially when they tossed around money like nothing.

Local legend states that during the early years many of the vacationing outlaws saddled up to the bar that is now Shipwrecked Pub. In fact, so many gangsters frolicked around the area that the bar became a favorite watering hole for the most famous bootlegger of all, Al Capone, who used his Door County trips as an opportunity to check on his ever-expanding business interests. During the reign of Prohibition many bootleggers sought out ways to hide their distribution of illegal liquor, and one of the more inventive solutions was to utilize a system of underground tunnels that not only made transporting liquor easier, but also allowed residents to discreetly travel to these marginally accepted hot spots. Directly underneath the pub are a series of old tunnels branching out to various locations all over town. It was rumored that Capone himself often used the tunnels to make fast getaways whenever the law raided the place. The tunnels are rife with legend, and perhaps the most infamous tells of two ambitious IRS agents that started poking around the bar looking for any evidence of Capone's misdealing. At a time when most people feared even giving Capone a sideways look, these foolhardy agents actively pursued him with vigor. To this day it is not known if the men succeeded in their quest, due to the fact that once they entered into the tunnels, they simple disappeared and were never heard from again. Like so many of the best legends, the credibility of this story cannot be verified, but it serves as a cautionary tale of the dangers of crossing a gangster—especially Al Capone. Unfortunately, due to safety concerns, the tunnels were sealed off many years ago, leaving their secrets forever buried.

Even more tantalizing tales revolve around several of Capone's illegitimate children who met their fate at the tavern. During the 1920s Capone was at the height of his power, and his infamy, prestige, and of course money attracted many disreputable women. These girls often worked as "ladies of the night" at the establishments Capone oversaw. One of Capone's Door County girls found herself in the unenviable position of carrying Capone's child. Going against the advice of those around her, the women chose to carry the child to birth. This critical lack of judgment inflamed Capone's monstrous temper as he confronted the woman, and a heated argument soon broke out. Shortly after the fight, like so many others around Capone, the young child simply went missing. Another torrid tale involves an illegitimate son of Capone. Many years ago it is said that Capone's son was a guest of the inn—that is until his lifeless body was found dangling from the end of a rope. Immediately after the grisly discovery, speculation rapidly spread that the son had taken his own life in a fit of severe depression. However, as time went by, townsfolk began to insinuate that perhaps the young man was "assisted" into death by one of his father's henchman. The rumor was that the young son had tired of the negative consequences that were tied to his heritage and he had made the ill-formed decision to work with the authorities and turn over evidence against his father. When word of the son's backstabbing plan reached the inner circle of Capone, the young man was swiftly dealt with and his "suicide" quickly followed.

Like any great nearly forgotten story, the truthfulness of these legends remains unsubstantiated. It is extremely likely that Capone did visit the area, either on vacation or business, along with many of his lesser known colleagues. Of course no records have surfaced tying any deaths of illegitimate children to Capone, but then again when it comes to the gangsters, secrecy was deemed an utmost quality, which makes any story about them possible.

Tommy Gun Adventures:
You can enjoy your own roaring 1920's evening by spending the night at the brew pub. Right upstairs they still have several lodging rooms where you can sleep easy knowing that the visiting gangsters are no longer downstairs.

MADISON, WI

SECRETS BURIED
WITHIN THE WONDER BAR

Secrets Buried Within the Wonder Bar

Location:

232 East Olin Avenue

Madison, WI 53713-1434

(608) 256-9430

Directions:

Take John Nolen Drive to the northwest and turn left onto East Olin Avenue; the Wonder Bar will be on your right side.

Gangster Lore:

The gangsters of the day seemed to really enjoy the Capitol City. Maybe with all the politicians in the city, the gangsters assumed they were not the most corrupt operators in Madison. Whatever the reason for their fondness, mobsters looked to Madison as a gateway for bringing their illegal enterprises to the Northwoods of Wisconsin and Minnesota. With so many outlaws passing through the area, the men needed some places to relax and enjoy some of the spoils of their labor. Luckily for them, the old Wonder Bar speakeasy provided everything they needed, including a human body dumping ground.

History:

1929 – Illinois bootlegger Roger "The Terrible" Touhy loaned money to his brother Eddie who constructed the building to be used as a speakeasy during Prohibition. The establishment was named The Wonder Bar.

1930s – Touhy sold the place to a group of three sisters who ran the establishment.

1948 – The bar was purchased by Mr. Kassak.

1970s – The bar and restaurant was bought by Dick Whalen, who changed the name to Whalen's Wonder Bar. It is during this period that the place became extremely popular.

1989 – Whalen sold his business to Michael O'Brian.

1990 – The business name was changed to the Madison Cigar Bar.

1992 – Michael O'Brian once again changed the name to the MOB Roadhouse, which played off of both the place's gangster history and the owner's initials.

1997 – The establishment became known as the Bar Next Door.

2003 – Friends Bruce and Denny purchased the place.

2009 – Jim Luedtke bought into the partnership and the name was changed to Luedtke's Wonder Bar.

Currently – The bar and restaurant is open for service.

Investigation:

The Wonder Bar is steeped in gangster history. Like so many Illinois bootleggers, Roger "The Terrible" Touhy was always on the lookout for new opportunities to distribute his illegal liquor. With endless profits coming in from his various "businesses," Touhy had no problem dishing out the money needed to construct the building. Although the style and ambiance of the building played an essential role in its design, it was the safety precautions that trumped everything else. During the 1920s, the speakeasy was positioned in the middle of nowhere. Surrounded by pasture and farmland, the turret design of the building not only appealed to the critical eye, it also provided a perfect lookout tower where guards could see for miles as they watched for any impending raids from the law. If any raid did sneak through the guards, the window sills throughout the building were constructed with the inventive feature of a flip-up hidden storage area where guns and other gear could be quickly disposed of. Those who would rather not get nabbed hanging out at a speakeasy could always escape through the underground tunnels that spider webbed out to the nearby lake. The tunnels also offered up the perfect cover to haul in and store a steady supply of illegal spirits. All of these precautions may seem a little over the top, but according to local legend, Touhy took the fortress idea a step further and was said to have insisted that the Wonder Bar be completely bomb-proof, a design point that thankfully has never been tested.

Once the security issues of the place were taken care of, Roger turned his attention to the important question of just exactly who would run the speakeasy. Roger had his hands full dealing with the deadly rival gang warfare that was exploding all over Illinois and he needed someone he could trust to attend to the bar's day-to-day operations. For this, Roger entrusted the operation of the new speakeasy to his brother Eddie. With Eddie running the show Roger could breathe a sigh of relief knowing that his sizeable new profits were secure. Adding to the Wonder Bar's cash inflow was the scattering of slot machines that ran through the main building. The atmosphere of the speakeasy was truly the embodiment of the roaring 1920s. On any given night the place was hopping with music, drinking, gambling, and dancing, all behaviors that lead to the bar's growing underworld reputation that attracted many unsavory characters.

There are numerous gangster legends that swirl around the Wonder Bar, including the speculation that many of the country's best known gangsters frequented the place. Besides Eddie, many of the Touhy gang members were counted among the regulars of the bar. It was a weird assortment of gamblers, bootleggers, hired muscle, and regular drinkers. It was said that when he was on positive terms with the Touhy gang, Al Capone and his henchman often were spotted inside the Wonder Bar. Although no

absolute proof of Capone's visits exist, at one point in the early days Capone was close to the Touhy gang, who worked with him distributing liquor. Their tenuous relationship would have provided the perfect opportunity for Capone and his underlings to visit the Wonder Bar. As the years passed and Capone rose up through the underworld, his relationship with the Touhy gang disintegrated, especially after Capone tried to have Roger Touhy killed. If the dates are right and the bar was not opened until 1929, a time when Capone was at war with the Touhy gang, it would seem unlikely that Capone would have ever set foot in the establishment. Several of the Wonder Bar staff informed me that Capone's connection to that place has been rumored for many decades. Capone was never one to document his every move, a fact that makes it nearly impossible for anyone to definitively place Capone at the Wonder Bar. However, it does makes for a great conversation while you belly up to the bar.

Perhaps the most infamous and grisly speakeasy story tells of a gangster who fell on hard times, and in his desperation turned to the Touhy gang for a loan to cover his obligations. Unable to keep up with the bone crushing interest payments, the gang decided to end both his misery, and his life. The story continues that in order to cover their tracks the gang stuffed his lifeless body into the wall of the Wonder Bar behind the second floor fireplace, where it still remains today. The staff informed me that the wall behind the fireplace has never been searched and that the fireplace itself was constructed only for show and not function, which only fires up the legend of some poor gangster rotting away inside the walls of the Wonder Bar. Touhy's former fortress has changed little over the years, as the owners have taken many steps to save the historic integrity of the building. Even today when you visit the Wonder Bar it is easy to let your mind drift back to the glory days of the 1930s, when on any given night the gangsters outnumbered the regular patrons. And while some believe that the gangsters have simply moved their headquarters down the road to the Capitol Building, their presence—and maybe even their bodies—will forever be attached to the infamous Wonder Bar.

CASE #4

OAKLAND, WI

ARTHUR DUNLOP'S LAST RIDE

Murdered Man
Found On Shore
Fremstad Lake

Body of unidentified ma

Arthur Dunlop's Last Ride

Location:

Fremsted Lake

Oakland, WI

North of Webster, WI

Directions:

The lake does not have a public access, so please view from the road.

From Webster, head north on Highway 35 for approximately five miles until you reach Old 35 Rd. on your right (it will be right across the road from Johnson Road on the left). Turn right onto Old 35 and it will immediately fork. You can go right on S. Fremsted Road, as it dead ends overlooking the lake. If you go left for ¼ mile, before you reach the turn for Fremsted Road you will be in the general area where Dunlop was killed.

There is also some confusion about the name of the lake itself. Newspapers of the day have it spelled as Frenstad, Fremstad, Fremsted, and Fernstad. In fact, the 1915 Burnett County plat book has the lake listed as Frensted. The 2010 Land Atlas and Plat Book spells it Fremsted. To muddle matters even more Google Maps has it listed as Fremstadt. For this case I have used the spelling of Fremsted, but feel free to join all the old newspapers and call it whatever you want.

Gangster Lore:
The Barker-Karpis gang was one of the deadliest group of outlaws operating in Minnesota and Wisconsin. The gang mostly consisted of brothers Fred and Doc Barker, and Alvin "Creepy" Karpis. Many other underworld characters were also utilized by the gang. The fact that they were also extremely fickle and impulsive only made them that much more dangerous. Never ones to shy away from shoot-outs and violence, the gang had gained a reputation as being no nonsense guys. To help aid them from the law the men traveled with their mother, Ma Barker, and believed that no one would expect that the nice young fellows traveling with their senior mother would be involved in such terrible criminal endeavors. Ma's boyfriend of the time, Arthur Dunlop, helped to fill out the perfect family picture. But like all families, everything was not perfect—a fact that would cost Arthur his life.

History:

1932 – Arthur Dunlop's naked body was discovered in Fremsted Lake in northern Wisconsin.

Investigation:

One of the biggest misconceptions in gangster history is the general public's widespread perception that Ma Barker was some gun-toting criminal mastermind that forced her sons into a life of unwanted crime. Although the legend made for a good cover story for the FBI after they killed the unarmed senior Barker in Florida, it could not have been further from the truth. While Ma got most of the notoriety in death, it was her sons that were the rabble rousers in life. There is no doubt that while Ma was at least somewhat aware of her sons' criminal behavior, she did not actively participate in it. Most who knew her reported that the rather unsophisticated southern woman was more interested in puzzles and music than robbing banks and kidnapping. Even though Ma wasn't much of an outlaw, she played an important role in the formation of the gang, as she served as the perfect cover story for the gang. It was much easier to blend in and avoid detection when the men traveled alongside their elderly mother, who they were lovingly caring for. With such a wonderful ruse in place the gang could focus more on their grand criminal plans.

In April of 1932, the Barker-Karpis gang was renting a home on Robert Street in St. Paul under the aliases of the Andersons. Ma Barker and her boyfriend, Arthur Dunlop, were living under the name Mr. and Mrs. George Anderson, while Fred Barker and Alvin "Creepy" Karpis claimed that they were traveling musicians. The group even went so far as to carry around a violin case to aid in the deception. The gang spent their days dutifully planning upcoming robberies of various Minneapolis banks. After a bank job was completed, the gang retreated to their safe haven and set about bigger plans. Unbeknownst to the gang, their true identities had been discovered by their landlady's son, who headed down to the police station with hopes of collecting the reward that was being offered for their capture. In a testament to the city's corruption, officials notified the gang of the trouble. Shortly after being identified, the gang haphazardly gathered their things and tore of out of St. Paul. The gang had no idea that their cover was blown by an article in *True Detective Magazine*. Instead, the men believed that it was the loose mouth of their mother's boyfriend that forced them out of hiding. While their assumption was wrong, the gang had good reason for making it; it was widely known that when drinking, Dunlop liked to let his mouth get really loose. Many times fellow gangsters overheard Dunlop spewing out confidential information about the gangs' operations. This was a dangerous liability that the gang could not afford or allow, even if it did come from their mother's boyfriend. After leaving St. Paul the men headed north toward Webster, Wisconsin—a ride that would seal Dunlap's fate.

On April 25, 1932, while cruising out of town, the gang pulled over around 2am and got out to once and for all silence the talkative Dunlop. The true specifics of the actual killing remain unknown, as many varying accounts of the death were published by the media. On Dunlop's death certificate the place of death was listed as "probably shot in car." The closest newspaper, the *Journal of Burnett County*, contradicted this version and wrote, "Officers state their belief that the man was killed after the car had been driven in on the old road. His upper lip was split from cheek to cheek, which was believed due from a blow when the man was taken from the car. It was while he was lying on the ground officers believe he was shot, as the earth there was said to be soaked with blood about 4 inches deep." The *La Crosse Tribune and Leader-Press* reported, "Sheriff Saunders said the body evidently had been dragged from an automobile to the lake shore, and added that apparently the man had not been killed at the scene where the body was found." It is important to note that during this period the Fremsted Lake area was in the middle of a severe drought, making the lake nothing more than a small pond surrounded by wet boggy areas. The *Journal of Burnett County* again carried all of the details in its April 28 edition:

> Examination of the roadway disclosed the
> fact that the murderers had driven their car
> on old highway 35, which travels closer to
> the lake than the new highway, a distance

of about 20 rods and after dragging the body from there to the edge of the lake had backed their car out the entire distance and turned south of highway No. 35, though they could have driven ahead on the old roadway about the same distance and reached the main road without using reverse. The plain imprint of four Goodyear tires led to the belief the rubbers were new. The apparent intention of those disposing of the body had been to throw it into the lake where it would not be discovered for some time, but the muddy edge prevented that and the dead man was left lying beyond the reach of the water. Men who recovered the body sunk in mud over their hip boots.

While the exact location of where the killing occurred is still disputed, one thing that is certain is that the gang unloaded three bullets into his body as he was dumped among the weedy pond bed. Dunlop's death certificate

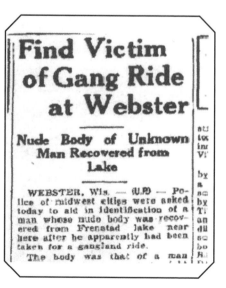

Find Victim of Gang Ride at Webster

Nude Body of Unknown Man Recovered from Lake

WEBSTER, Wis. — (U.P) — Police of midwest cities were asked today to aid in identification of a man whose nude body was recovered from Frenstad lake near here after he apparently had been taken for a gangland ride.

The body was that of a man

lists the cause of death as "murdered by shooting. Three (3) bullet wounds thru the right chest." The *Journal of Burnett County* expanded on the wounds: "The fatal shots entered the right breast of the man and came out on the left side of his spine."

At 9am, Frank Scotka, who resided on the lake, was returning from a trip to the Yellow Lake store when he discovered Dunlop's body. The *Rhinelander Daily News* reported on the find claiming, "The body was that of a man about 55 years old, five feet eight inches in height, and weighed 150 pounds. He had iron gray hair, a neatly trimmed mustache, and was slightly bald." The *Journal of Burnett County* wrote, "The body was entirely nude and buttons lying on the lake shore indicated that the clothes had been ripped from their victim." Breaking from their usual thoroughness, the gang left quite a few clues for the police to discover. While Dunlop's body had no marks of identification, several guns were discarded at the scene. The *Sheboygan Press* wrote that "two revolvers, one .38 caliber and the other .45 caliber were lying near the body." Soon other details started to emerge. An exploded .44 or .45 caliber bullet was found in the pool of Dunlop's blood. Three days after the discovery of the body authorities found a blood soaked glove three miles away on nearby Highway 35. The *Wisconsin State Journal* wrote that this new find pushed authorities "to seek a woman as the murderer."

Right from the start the authorities blamed the killing on gangland operators. Dunlop's death certificate listed his occupation as "Unknown. Suspected underworld character." The *Wisconsin State Journal's* headline for the story was "find victim of gang ride at Webster." The *Sheboygan Press* reported that "Sheriff (Charles) Saunders expressed the opinion the man had been taken for a 'ride.'" The police knew that if the killing was gangster related they would need some assistance in finding the murderer so they sent the crime photos and victim fingerprints to offices in Chicago, Milwaukee, Duluth, and St. Paul, in hopes of an identification. The body was originally thought to be that of Minneapolis underworld character John McTague who had just skipped out on a $20,000 bond. Even Dunlop's death certificate lists him as George Dunlop, Sr.

While it is quite certain that the Barker-Karpis gang members were the ones responsible for ending Dunlop's life, researcher Paul Maccabee wrote about an interesting denial his book *John Dillinger Slept Here.* Maccabee wrote that when interviewed many years later, Alvin Karpis claimed the gang was not responsible for Dunlop's death, and unapologetically looked to shift the blame to one of many within the underworld that would have liked to have seen Dunlop dead. Even with his halfhearted denial the evidence against Karpis kept growing. According to the *Journal of Burnett County,* on the very same day that Dunlop's body was discovered, a suspicious gang "drove to the Anderson Bros filling station and bought gas and oil. They occupied a ford coach and were accompanied by a woman driving another car of the same make... They inquired of Anderson (gas attendant) how they might drive to Danbury without using highways NO. 70, 85, or county trunk D, and were directed north across the meadow line." When shown an issue of True Detective Magazine—the same magazine that got the gang noticed in St. Paul—gas station attendants John Sandberg and Elfred Anderson identified the men as Fred Barker and Alvin Karpis. Other witnesses

reported seeing the fleeing men in Danbury. The gang was also spotted just west of the Interstate Bridge, just before they disappeared near Hinckley, MN. On May 5, the *Journal of Burnett County* ran the photos of Alvin Karpis and Fred Barker on their front page as being the prime suspects.

PIPE, WI

AL CAPONE HANGS OUT IN PIPE

Al Capone Hangs Out in Pipe

Location:

Capone's of Pipe Restaurant

N10302 US Hwy 151

Malone, WI 53049

(920) 795-4140

http://www.caponesofpipe.com

Directions:

Although the postal address is Malone, Capone's of Pipe can be found right on Highway 151 in Pipe, WI.

Gangster Lore:

One of the problems with researching gangsters is that many of the places that are tied to them have been lost to time, or they have been so significantly changed that the original structure is utterly unrecognizable. Many of the banks they robbed are no longer banks, hotels where they hid out are now parking lots, and speakeasies where they danced the night away have been converted into upscale condominiums. With the ever increasing march of progress we continually lose our historic treasures. Even more depressing is seeing some of these old places that were once pillars of the community simply rot away as they sit empty, relegated to the lowly function of providing a constant reminder of better days long since passed. Try not to get too discouraged though because among the list of lost memories reside places where history is not forgotten. Nowhere is this more evident than at Capone's of Pipe Restaurant. From the minute you walk into this 150-year-old building, you feel as though you stepped back into the 1920s, so be sure to keep an eye out, because at an old gangster hot spot like this, you never know who might be stopping by for a drink.

History:

1846 – Two years before Wisconsin became a state, Henry Fuhrman constructed the three-story building to serve as a stagecoach inn. Serving mostly travelers, the business was complete with boarding rooms, a full bar, and a restaurant. The establishment was known as Fuhrman's Hotel.

1920s – Like so many other speakeasies around the country the hotel/saloon functioned as a house of ill repute where ladies of the night "entertained" the clientele.

1920s-30s – The bar and restaurant was said to be a frequent stopping point for notorious bootlegger Al Capone and many other gangsters as they passed through the area on their way up north.

1941 – Owner Wally Manderscheid renovated the building by removing a hall and staircase. To help modernize the building, indoor toilets were also added.

1950s-1970s – The building changed hands quite often and a progression of new owners tried their luck at running a restaurant.

1976 – Owners Ed and Toni Brandenburg threw a party to celebrate the property being listed as a Wisconsin Historical Landmark. During this time the widely known restaurant was called Club Harbor.

1980 – The building was added to the National Register of Historic Places.

1980s-2000s – The historic landmark sat empty as it slowly fell into disrepair. Several plans to utilize the building fell through, leaving the building as an eye sore among the community.

2004 – Tom Knecht purchased the dilapidated building with the lofty renovation plan of restoring it to its original grandeur. Having sat empty for over 20 years, the renovation proved to be a monumental task. All three floors were stripped to their studs while all new drywall, electrical, and plumbing was installed.

2005 – The establishment re-opened as Capone's of Pipe, paying homage to the building's gangster past.

Currently – The bar and restaurant is open to the public.

Investigation:

When you walk inside Capone's of Pipe you can easily imagine it as a popular hangout for the underworld characters of our past. With a bullet-ridden 1948 Chevy anchoring the dance floor, and a life-size figure of Al Capone keeping a watchful eye on things from the corner, you may want to be sure that you sit with your back to the wall. I spoke with Tom Knecht, who is the current owner of Capone's of Pipe and the one responsible for bringing the building back to life. Tom recanted the struggles and triumphs of completely gutting the building as he looked to resurrect the historic building from the grips of neglect. Tom also shared with me many of the surviving legends from the building's sorted past.

During the 1920s the inn served as a speakeasy/brothel where men could go to gamble, drink, dance, and even partake in one of the "ladies of the night" that worked there. Many of these speakeasies were positioned on the outskirts of town, far away from the prying eyes of both the law and curious do-gooders. It was also not uncommon for brothels of the time to attract some rather unsavory characters. At Capone's, the legend of a murder taking place inside the old brothel has been floating around for many years. Like most great legends, the details are a bit vague, but the story goes that back in the heyday of the speakeasy, a young prostitute was murdered inside the brothel by one of her disreputable clients. Who this unnamed woman was has never been discovered, and of course the murder has never been verified, which only increases the frequency by which it is repeated, and enhances its intrigue among those with a macabre sense of curiosity.

Another main legend of Capone's states that during the 1920s and 30s, the old speakeasy was a popular hot spot for traveling gangsters to stop off for a quick drink or two before heading off up north on vacation. And throughout the late 1920s, gangsters did not get any bigger than Al 'Scarface' Capone. It is alleged that Capone and his colleagues often frequented the establishment on their numerous excursions up north. In Wisconsin, there is a never ending list of places that claim to have been Capone's favorite hideout, and although it is nearly impossible to pin down every place Scarface visited, we can make some general assumptions. The unique location of Capone's of Pipe puts it straight in the path that Capone would have taken as he hightailed it out of Chicago to the seclusion of Wisconsin's Northwoods. We know that Capone often visited his 'hideout' cabin in Couderay – making a pit stop in Pipe a likely scenario. The restaurant's location would have been convenient for Al to pass through on his way to see his brother Ralph, who lived for many years in Mercer, WI. It is also entirely plausible that Capone and others stopped in Pipe on their trips up to Door County, which is another alleged hot spot for gangsters. While Capone may have been the most well-known gangster of his time, he certainly would not have been the only one to have frequented the bar. Local legends tell of several residents who operated stills for the Capone bootlegging business. If the legends are to be believed, this would have necessitated a visit from several of Capone's men to collect the moonshine and/or money, and they most certainly would have not passed up an opportunity to enjoy the speakeasy.

Adding even more credibility to the Capone legend is the fact that several eye witnesses recall running into Capone while he was at the speakeasy. Former newspaper columnist, Langdon Divers, wrote of his 1930s childhood run-in with the infamous gangster. Divers was riding his bike with a friend when their thirst got the best of them and they made a pit stop at Club Harbor (Capone's of Pipe) to get something to drink. Divers remembered seeing a group of men inside the bar and ended up talking to the one with scars on his face. At the time, young Divers had no idea just who he was speaking with; it wasn't until a few weeks later when he learned the real identity of the talkative stranger. If the gentleman Divers ran into was truly Al Capone, the encounter would have had to have taken place before 1932, the year that Capone was shipped off to prison.

While all of the gangsters who roamed Wisconsin are long dead, Capone's of Pipe does a marvelous job at recreating the feeling of the era in which they lived. Surrounded by an old whiskey still, and a variety of pistols and Tommy Guns on the wall, it is all too easy to picture yourself back in the Roaring 20s. While you dig into your pizza you can take great pride in knowing that you are keeping alive the long standing tradition of interesting characters hanging out at Capone's.

COUDERAY, WI

AL CAPONE'S
NORTHWOOD HIDEOUT

Capone's Northwoods Hideout

Location:
12101 W County Rd CC
Couderay, WI 54828
(The future of the hideout is unknown and it may still be
private land, so please check before going.)

Directions:
From Couderay, WI, Highway 70 (27) go north on County
Hwy CC and follow it until it forks with County Hwy N.
Stay to the right on Hwy CC and head to the east, the Hide-
out will be on your right. The main lodge is set back away
from the road.

Gangster Lore:
It seems like you cannot throw a rock in Wisconsin without
hitting some place that is rumored to have had attachments

to Al Capone. Nearly every community in the state boasts legends of Capone frequenting their town. From hotels and restaurants, to brothels and resorts, if all the legends are to be believed, Capone was the world's busiest traveler. Yet, among all of these speculations as to Capone's whereabouts, one place stands out among the rest as being Al's favorite hangout in Wisconsin, and that place is aptly named the Hideout.

History:

1925 – Capone began buying up property in the Northwoods along Cranberry Lake.

1928 – Capone had workers begin construction on his Northwoods retreat. The main lodge was built with protection in mind as evidenced by the 18-inch thick cement walls. Capone spared no expense on the project with the hideout construction costing over $25,000. The *Oshkosh Daily Northwestern* reported that the land was purchased in the name of George Bonesch.

1959 – The property was purchased from the Capone estate by Guy and Jean Houston for a reported sum of 4.25 million dollars. The couple opened the establishment as a tourist destination.

2009 – After nearly 50 years of operation, the Hideout finally closed down and went into foreclosure. The foreclosed property was put onto the real estate market and received extensive national media coverage. When no bids for the infamous property surfaced, the Chippewa Valley Bank of Wisconsin took ownership of the property for $2.6 million.

2009 – The Lac Courte Oreilles tribe purchased the land from the bank.

2010 – The fate of the former Hideout tourist attraction is not known.

Investigation:

In the late 1920s, gangsters did not get more well-known than Al Capone. As Chicago's largest bootlegger, Capone's infamy reached throughout the country. Living such a dangerous and stressful life, Capone sought out the safety and seclusion of the Northwoods. After scouring the area, Capone purchased a 400-acre plot of land in Couderay. The tranquil surroundings provided Capone with the perfect retreat where he entertained many of his criminal guests and business partners. The heavily forested land of the area ensured that the gangster would remain hidden, free to pursue his personal interests. A 1929 *Miami Daily News* article reported, "This Wisconsin spot is said to be ideal for the gang leader, being surrounded on all sides by dense woods and with roads leading in all directions in case sudden flight is necessary."

The main lodge was decorated in an elegant Northwoods décor. Grand antler chandeliers and light fixtures were offset by the most modern conveniences money could buy. Matching spiral staircases showcased the inside of the lodge, which also included a majestic fireplace to keep visitors toasty during the cold Wisconsin winters. The fact that Capone spared no expense on the design and furnishings guaranteed that visitors would have been treated to a lavish, yet rustic, vacation at the Hideout. Although Capone banked on the area's remoteness to provide security, he did not rely on it completely. The first thing you notice upon entering the Hideout is the old stone gun tower where armed guards were once perched high above the ground, overlooking the entrances to the hideout. At the time, the guards would have had a clear sight to the road, ensuring that anyone not invited to the hideout, would experience an unfriendly welcoming. The construction of the main lodge also showed evidence of Capone's safety concerns, as the walls of the building were enforced by 18 inches of concrete. Capone even had special holes placed in the walls where machine guns could be mounted.

To the normal person the overabundance of security on the property seems a bit overdone, yet in Capone's line of work neglecting these precautions could end up being deadly.

Adhering to this philosophy Capone also constructed a one-room jail house behind the cabin. The official use of the building is unknown, but speculation falls on it being a place where Capone's enemies were held, and eventually 'persuaded' to see things Capone's way.

Nestled back behind the estate is the beautiful Blueberry Lake, a 37-acre private pond and beach that is steeped in gangster lore. Legend states that Capone used the lake to further his illegal bootlegging business. Planes filled with Canadian liquor would fly in and land on the lake where the merchandise could easily be loaded onto trucks to be distributed throughout the Midwest. Former tour guides of the Hideout told the cautionary tale that those who did not learn their lesson in Capone's jail often met their watery grave at the bottom of the lake. One can only wonder what grisly secrets would be revealed if the lake was ever drained.

The question of how much time Capone actually spent at the Hideout is still hotly debated. Many newspapers of the day report that his main lodge was not completed until late 1928 or early 1929. Capone himself spent nine months of 1929 in a cell at Philadelphia's

Eastern State Penitentiary on a weapons charge. After being released from jail Capone's freedom did not last long, and he was again arrested and sent to Alcatraz Prison in 1932. This timeline of events dramatically limits the amount of time Capone could have spent at the Hideout. Yet on the flip side, the fact that his brother, Ralph Capone, lived for quite a while in nearby Mercer would have provided Al with some incentive to frequently visit his summer retreat. Even if Capone wasn't continually at the lodge, the stories of planes flying in moonshine would have necessitated the visit of his criminal colleagues. While it is certain that Capone did visit the lodge, the question of just how many times he was there will have to go unanswered.

Tommy Gun Adventures:
You can still visit the area, but the ultimate fate of the Hideout is not known. It was purchased by the Lac Courte Oreilles Tribe in 2010. Their plans for the property are not known, and my numerous inquires with them went unanswered. Unfortunately, it appears that before being foreclosed upon the former owners gutted the lodge of nearly all of its historic items.

Lake Geneva, WI

Bugs Moran and Many Other Mobsters at Watersedge

Bugs Moran and Many Other Mobsters at Watersedge B&B

Location:

Watersedge Bed and Breakfast

W4232 West End Road

Lake Geneva, WI 53147

(262) 425-9845

www.watersedgebb.com

Directions:

From downtown take Highway 50 to the west for approximately four miles. Turn right on Red Chimney Road. Take your 1st left on West End Road and the inn will be on your right. The Watersedge is right next door to the French Country Inn.

Gangster Lore:

If you were a gangster traveling through Wisconsin in the 1920s and 1930s, you certainly would have been familiar with the inn on Lake Como. There were not too many places where you could hide out and relax without a curious owner snooping in on your business. The fact that the owner asked few questions, and respected ever fewer laws, made it a safe haven for gangsters. Even though the gangster days are long behind us, the historic inn still remains a must-not-miss location.

History:

1895 – The area was a dairy farm that was attached to the old icehouse to make a permanent residence.

1920s – The home was purchased by Hobart Hermanson who converted the dwelling, along with the Lake Como Inn, into a full-scale resort. Hermanson also owned a lot of other properties in Lake Geneva.

1960 – Tired of the resort business, Hermanson simply boarded up the building and moved down to Florida. The place remained boarded up for several years.

1984 – The property was purchased by Sven and Newell Friedman. The Friedmans were interior designers who decided to convert the property into a B&B.

2001 – Marge and Dom Trumfio purchased the property. The couple then set about the laborious process of renovating the property, spending over $500,000 in the process.

Currently – The B&B is open to the public.

Investigation:

The Watersedge B&B was part of the original Lake Como Inn property owned by Hobart Hermanson. During the early years of the business both the Watersedge and French Country Inn were combined into Hermanson's business that incorporated lodging, gambling, dining, dancing, and drinking. Many of the vacationing gangsters would spend the night here while eating next door at what is now the French Country Inn. The laundry list of past guests reads like the FBI Most Wanted list…including Baby Face Nelson, Tommy Carroll, John Paul Chase, Bugs Moran, and John Dillinger.

One of the most intriguing aspects of the entire inn is the room aptly known as the Bugs Moran Suite. At first glance the room appears just like any other spacious upscale B&B room. Yet a more thorough inspection leads to the discovery that the room is a virtual Fort Knox. Hermanson was known as the slot machine baron of the area, and had gambling machines scattered throughout the entire region. Back in the 1920s and 1930s the room was designated as the "counting room" where all the change collected from the gaming machines would be tallied up. Needless to say, with the extraordinary amounts of money passing through the room, increased security was essential. The walls of the room are lined with 15-inch thick concrete reinforcement that would make breaking in nearly impossible. The windows are protected with bars, and the addition of a secret entrance anchored by a heavy duty door all combined to make the room virtually impenetrable. If personal safety is a concern for you, then this suite will not disappoint you.

The aforementioned suite received its name due to the ties George "Bugs" Moran had with the inn. Moran, a well-known bootlegging competitor of Al Capone spent a lot of time enjoying the comforts of the inn. Moran would do all his lodging at the inn, and when he got  hungry he would venture next door to get his meals. In her article, *Gangster Getaways*, Andria Hayday writes this of Moran's visits: "Locals still pass along tales of how he would arrive with a phalanx of bodyguards and sit down to eat with his back to the corner, requesting a certain wait-ress with the gumption to serve him." After the St. Valen-tine's Day Massacre, Moran's wife, Lucille, was said to have left him in order to spend her life with Hermanson. Lucille moved into the inn, and began her duties as man-ager of the speakeasy.

Outside of the obvious gangster connections, the historic inn also possesses many secrets, and several fascinating components remain hidden just one level beneath the main floor. The owners discovered that underneath the main floor was where the high action gambling area was located. This part of the building was used as a speakeasy where guests could try their luck at slot machines, craps, poker, and several other games of chance. On any given night you could find the boisterous speakeasy filled with patrons gambling while drinking and enjoying the comforts of a woman. To help ensure privacy at the speakeasy, all of the windows were cemented closed. Outside of the gambling room sits the old vault and safe where the gambling profits were kept. In her article, *Gangster Getaways*, Andria Hayday tells of an elderly neighbor who recalled rigging "slot machines as boy, and once stumbled across a man bleeding from gunshot wounds in the dead of night." The wonderfully placed B&B rests directly on Lake Como and many of the rooms showcase breathtaking views of the water. Legend states that many of the old slot machines were simply dumped into Lake Como, where they sit today in their watery grave. The long old table that Hermanson used inside his counting room to keep track of his profits has been fittingly relocated to the old gambling room.

Not too far from the gambling room rests the old garage that originally attached the two parts of the building. What is unique about this garage is that it contains a concrete ramp running from the outside directly down to the open basement. This architectural anomaly did not occur by accident or error, as it was well designed to serve an impor-

tant purpose. During Prohibition, the biggest risk facing
bootleggers was the possible detection of their activities by
law enforcement agents. To combat this threat, many
underground tunnels were created throughout towns and
communities where the illegal liquor could be discreetly
smuggled. To protect the inn from the authorities' prying
eyes, the ramp was constructed so vehicles could quickly
drive right into the safety of the basement. Once away from
curious onlookers, barrels of whisky and moonshine could
be easily rolled onto the ramp and loaded into the waiting
cars.

As I drove up to the inn, I chuckled at the appropriate-
ness of its location. The inn itself is tucked away off the
main road hidden from sight. Unless you were specifically
searching for it, you would not find it. I could understand
why this type of seclusion would have been appealing to
the outlaws. Once inside, I was surprised by the amount of

living history within its walls. Each room amazingly revealed another gangster secret that had been painstakingly preserved. The place contained old money counting tables, hidden entrances to rooms, cash vaults, an old speakeasy, bars on the windows, and even the possibility of finding discarded slot machines in the lake. The place truly covers everything the modern gangster tourist needs.

Tommy Gun Adventure:

Follow in the footsteps of the most infamous criminals of the 1920s and 30s by spending some time relaxing at the inn. The inn has all your safety needs covered, so feel free to leave your Tommy Guns in the car.

LAKE GENEVA, WI

GANGSTERS' PARADISE
AT THE FRENCH COUNTRY INN

Gangsters' Paradise
at the French Country Inn

Location:
French Country Inn
W4190 West End Road
Lake Geneva, WI 53147
(262) 245–5220
www.frenchcountryinn.com

Directions:

From downtown take Highway 50 to the west for approximately four miles. Turn right on Red Chimney Road. Take your 1st right on West End Road and the inn will be right in front of you.

Gangster Lore:

Lake Geneva has always been a popular haven for mobsters who were looking for a quick escape into Wisconsin's countryside. A mere twelve miles from the Illinois border, the quaint little town provided the perfect getaway for those who truly needed to get away. Starting the 1920s, and continuing into the 30s, this little resort town played host to some of the most dangerous men in the country. Luckily for you, many of the same resorts they stayed at are still there for you to explore.

History:

1880s – The exquisite building was constructed in Denmark. The craftsmanship was so fine that the building was shipped over to the U.S. to be showcased at the 1893 Chicago's World Fair.

1900s – Once the fair had run its course, the buildings were sold off. The Danish building was purchased and shipped up to the resort town of Lake Geneva. The building functioned as the private residence for the Knotters family, who often entertained friends and family at their upscale home.

1920s – The private home was purchased by Hobart Hermanson who converted the dwelling into a full-scale resort. Hermanson began calling the place the Lake Como Inn. He also owned the property that is now known as Watersedge B&B.

1960 – Tired of the resort business, Hermanson simply boarded up the building and moved down to Florida. The place remained boarded up for several years.

1970 – With Hermanson relaxing in Florida, the inn was

sold to new owners. Along with the change in ownership came the re-naming of the business. The place was known as The Red Chimney.

1981 – The Red Chimney was purchased by Sam Argento, who had grand dreams of beginning the laborious restoration effort needed to return the building to its former glory. Argento also reverted the resort's name back to Lake Como Inn.

1986 – After Argento's renovation plans failed, the place sat empty for several years. Finally the historic building was purchased by Tom Navilio, who also embarked on the monumental task of restoring the home. This time though, the work was completed and the inn was transformed back to its Danish heritage.

Currently – The inn and restaurant is open to the public.

Investigation:

During the roaring 1920s and 30s, Hobart Hermanson ran the Lake Como Inn which included the property and buildings that are now owned separately by the French Country Inn and the Watersedge B&B. Under Prohibition, Hermanson earned a nice little profit by operating his place as a speakeasy. He mainly ran the place as a legit business, since no one except the Federal Government really considered providing liquor a criminal offense. Like many other business owners of the time, Hermanson seemed to frequently teeter on both sides of the law. While not breaking any major laws, he wasn't completely squeaky clean either, as he would often provide secluded private rooms for those special clients who were obviously on the lam. Hermanson also operated many gambling machines throughout the area, counting his profits at the Watersedge B&B. His ability to accommodate these underworld characters provided the Lake Como Inn with a reputation of being a gangster-friendly resort. That type of label opened the flood gates for some of the country's most wanted men to turn the place into their own personal vacation grounds.

The roaring 1920s brought with it a time of corruption and lawlessness that to this day remains unequaled. Prohibition was a Godsend to aspiring criminals looking for a career boost. Alongside bootlegging came gambling, prostitution, and a plethora of additional illegal activities that swiftly lined the pocket books of the mobsters. With money coming in from all directions, gangsters found Lake Geneva's resorts conducive to their newfound lifestyles. Legend states that nearly every big name gangster of the time spent some time in town. The list of traveling gangsters passing through the area is truly impressive. Notorious Chicago bootlegger George "Bugs" Moran relaxed next door at the Watersedge B&B. Al Capone was frequently spotted around town, albeit not anywhere near Bugs. The 1930s brought no shortages of gangsters either. Bank robbers John Paul Chase and Homer Van Meter were said to have spent some time at the inn. It got so popular that even Public Enemy #1, John Dillinger, was rumored to have gotten cozy with the resorts of Lake Geneva.

Things really got hot in June of 1934, when two happy couples checked into the Lake Como Inn. The first couple was given a remote room inside the main house, and guests reported that they mostly kept to themselves. While the first couple had decided to lay low, the second  couple more than made up for their counterparts' absence. This jovial young couple darted around the restaurant and tavern, easily talking and mixing with the other vacationing guests. Days were spent out shopping and touring, while the couple spent their nights eating, drinking, and dancing the night away inside the inn. Little did the guests know that they had become rooming mates with two of the country's most dangerous and wanted men. The rarely seen man tucked away in his room was Tommy Carroll, who was kept busy with his girlfriend, Jean Delaney. The gentleman who spent his time mingling with the others was George "Baby Face" Nelson, who contrary to his reputation as a hot tempered killer, could effortlessly woo even the toughest of crowds. In fact, in their book, *Baby Face*

Nelson, authors Steven Nickels and William Helmer wrote that Nelson and his wife, Helen, had "given the impression that they were young newlyweds." Not exactly the charm you would expect from a stone cold killer. After a few days of living the good life, Carroll and his girlfriend made plans to head up to St. Paul to refuel his arsenal. After saying goodbye to Nelson, Carroll eagerly checked out. It would be Carroll's last stay at the inn, and a few days later he would be gunned downed by police in Waterloo, Iowa. After hearing the devastating news of Carroll's death, Nelson too departed from the inn, but unlike Carroll, the inn would still play major role in Nelson's future.

Having grown so attached to the inn, Nelson surprisingly made arrangements with Hermanson to return to the inn to spend some downtime during the upcoming winter. Nelson was a master of eluding the police through deception and unpredictability, so it was completely out of character for him so openly announce any specific plans. Doing so at the inn demonstrated the trust he felt in Hermanson. Unbeknownst to Nelson, the Feds had also learned of his vacation plans through several captured colleagues. It didn't take long for the authorities to trace Nelson back to the Lake Como Inn. A 1936 *Denton Journal* article wrote, "In the course of this investigation, a hotel keeper at Lake Geneva, Wis., told F.B.I. agents he suspected that some previous guests at his hotel were members of the Dillinger gang."

After confirming Hermanson's account of gangsters inhabiting his hotel, the FBI discovered the location of Baby Face's return to Lake Geneva. With Hermanson's cooperation with the law, it appears that Nelson's trust in him

was unwarranted. However, for his part, Hermanson was most likely threatened that if he did not cooperate, he would be sent to prison for harboring known criminals. Immediately agents were sent to stake out Hermanson's inn. Daily life for the agents consisted of slowly watching a steady parade of vacationers and visitors stop by the inn. This monotony dragged on for several weeks with no sign of the elusive Nelson. Then, just as their hopes of Nelson's return had started to diminish, another car began to approach the inn. With the Hermanson's away for the weekend, the agents were the sole caretakers of the inn. What happened next is told in several different versions. In his book, *Public Enemies*, Bryan Burrough wrote that when Baby Face pulled up the agents were caught off-guard because they had believed the car belonged to the returning Hermanson family. As the car pulled in from the long driveway, Nelson left the engine running as he inquired as to the whereabouts of Hermanson. With his wife next to him, and John Paul Chase in the backseat, Nelson quickly smelled a trap and took off out of the inn before the Feds figured out their mistake. Immediately after his departure, the agents pieced together his identity and hurriedly called in the report to Chicago. Baby Face calmly made his way through downtown Lake Geneva. The *Denton Journal* covered the story writing that "as the car containing the trio passed through Lake Geneva a few moments later, an agent on assignment there recognized Nelson in the driver's seat and also noted the tag numbers. He too phoned Chicago."

The media told a different version of the event, implying that group got out of their car and walked up to the front door. The *Denton Journal* wrote, "In the absence of the hotel man, the agents at the house saw a V-8 sedan stop in front of the house. Two men and a woman were in it. The visitors, whose identities could not be determined by the agents, left quickly after getting no immediate response from their knock." Seemingly getting their stories from numerous sources, the *Chicago Evening American* wrote that "two agents approached the cottage. As they did so, Mrs. Gillis and a man whose identity is unknown fled by a rear door and escaped in a car toward Chicago." How could so many newspapers print such varying accounts of the incident? Perhaps the reason lies with the FBI. During this time the FBI was becoming a true master at manipulating the media to spin their version of events. In order to save face in the eye of the general public, it is conceivable that instead of admitting that Nelson once again outwitted them, they spun the story in their favor. The official government version even went so far as to deny that Nelson was even in Lake Geneva, as evidenced by the *Reno Evening Gazette* which wrote, "Another rumor was that Nelson had been in a hideout near Lake Geneva, Wis., just before the fatal gun fight in Barrington, Ill. This was denied by H.M. Glegg, official of the department of justice who came from Washington to direct the hunt for the remnants of the Dillinger gang."

Regardless of the conflicting versions of the story, the visit to Hermanson's Inn was Nelson's last. While hightailing it back to Chicago, Nelson engaged the Feds in a bloody gunfight that ended up talking the life of two federal agents. A day later, Nelson's bullet-ridden dead body was discovered as well.

The old Lake Como Inn is now the beautifully restored French Country Inn. I was given a tour of the historic inn and got to spend some time wandering the same areas that many of the world's most infamous gangsters did so many years ago. Although the place has been thoroughly renovated, the owners paid dutiful attention to the original plans of the inn. A visit to the inn doesn't require any imagination to make you feel like you are transported back to when Bugs Moran and Baby Face vacationed here.

Tommy Gun Adventures:

Relive the glory days of the 1920s and 30s by spending the night at the inn. While here make sure you travel around the charming downtown area just like all the gangsters did. Just be sure that no federal agents are watching you.

WINTER, WI

THE CAUTIONARY TALE
OF JOE SALTIS

The Cautionary Tale of Joe Saltis

Location:

Barker Lake Lodge

6821 W Golf Course Rd.

Winter, WI 54896

(715) 266-4050

www.barkerlakelodge.com

Directions:

From Winter, WI, (Highway 70) head north on Co. Hwy. W, which will turn into Barker Lake Rd. Turn left on Golf Course Rd and follow it to the lodge.

Gangster Lore:

Having traveled all over the U.S in search of the history of gangsters, I thought I had seen it all. From walking along Ma Barker's death site in Florida to holding the picnic basket

Baby Face Nelson used to shield his Tommy Gun, I was acquainted with places that preserved their history, yet when I drove up to Barker Lake Lodge I was truly amazed. Here in the middle of Wisconsin's Northwoods sits a perfectly preserved gangster resort. I hate to write in clichés, but with vintage guest rooms, gangster antiques, and a few stray bullet holes, this place really has to be seen in order to be believed.

History:

1929- Chicago beer baron Joe Saltis purchased the Northwoods land and began construction on a grand lodge. Taking over one year to complete the lodge's enormous cost was estimated at over $100,000. The property contained the main two-story lodge, several guest cabins, and even a nine-hole golf course.

1930- Saltis looked to get out of the bootlegging business and "retired" to the peace and quiet of his Northwoods cabin.

1947- At the age of 53, complications from a stomach ulcer took the life of Saltis in a Chicago hospital.

1950-2000- The lodge passed through several owners. The golf course became a separate business from the lodge and cabins.

2000- David Palmer purchased the property.

Currently- The historic lodge is available year round for families, groups, special events, and individuals looking for a unique lodging experience.

Investigation:

The Barker Lake Lodge takes pride in providing guests
with a truly unique vacation experience. I met with the
lodge owner, David Palmer, who gave me a tour of the
property. To his credit, David has researched much of the
gangster history of his place, which makes for an interesting tour. A cedar log interior clings to the walls as you
venture through the great room, dining hall, and game
room. Of course being a former bootlegger's hangout the
lodge even had its own bar. Upstairs the lodge boasts nine
guest rooms that are magnificently decorated just as they
would have been back when visiting gangsters stayed the
night. Adding to the historic charm of the place are several
bullet holes that adorn the walls and help transport visitors
back to a simpler time. Back to a time when a wealthy Chicago gangster invested an ungodly amount of money into a
beautiful Wisconsin resort only to see it all slip away after
the repeal of Prohibition. Luckily for you, Joe Saltis' loss
was your gain.

"Polack" Joe Saltis was a beer baron from Chicago who
took advantage of Prohibition and began providing boot-
leg liquor to his thirsty patrons. Competing with the likes
of Al Capone and George 'Bugs' Moran, Saltis was often
described in the newspapers as the cruelest gangster in
Chicago, which flies in stark contrast to his self-proclaimed
moniker, "Gentleman Joe Saltis." Regardless of what
people called him, Saltis soon grew tired of the dangerous

life and looked to the Northwoods of Wisconsin to escape both his past, and more importantly, the authorities.

In 1928, a posse of law enforcement agents set out to Wisconsin to capture Saltis. The *Milwaukee Journal* wrote that "a Federal posse set out to get Saltis in his Barker Lake quarters, but he escaped in a motorboat, and for seven months he played hide and seek with the law. He was chased all over Wisconsin and sought in Florida as well." In November of 1930, Saltis' fourteen-year-old son was involved in an accident in Chicago and was rushed to the hospital. This odd twist of fate forced Saltis out of his Northwoods sanctuary and back into the fires of Chicago, where he was still a wanted man. Knowing that the law would be waiting for him in Chicago, the *Evening Huron-ite*, reported that Saltis was looking to make a deal. "'I'll surrender to the law,' he told James Burke, his attorney, 'but I'd like a chance to make bond. I want to be with my boy, but I don't want to disgrace him by being arrested in the same room with him.'"

Much like Capone, Saltis took his safety and security seriously, during his tenure at the lodge there were three gun towers on the property to help ensure that no unwanted visitors made it to the lodge. The *Milwaukee Journal* wrote that "the Barker lake hide-out was built just so. It was equipped with all the modern equipment and it could, in a pinch, have, served as a fortress." Saltis' estate was truly all-encompassing; the lodge contained several sleeping rooms, a majestic bar, and even a large gambling hall where you could try your luck on the various slot machines. Even though the lodge provided endless entertainment, there was even more to do outside. The property boasted a private golf course boarded by a fenced in park that was chalk full of deer and other native animals. Tucked behind the golf course was an illegal still that provided liquor for Saltis and his guests. There was so much activity at the lodge that at one point Saltis employed the majority of small town's residents. During his court trial, the *Wisconsin State Journal* recorded Saltis' speech to the judge. "'Nobody has done more for Wisconsin than Joe Saltis', Saltis said. 'I've spent $100,000 during the depression to keep men at work at my place at Barker Lake. I've stocked the lake with 50,000,000 fish. I stocked the land with 5,000 pheasants, and gave my neighbors 10,000 more for their land. It costs me $500 a year to feed the birds. I've brought partridges in here too. I have 30 deer and I'm breeding more and 120 silver foxes.'"

Although the Northwoods sheltered Saltis from the Chicago authorities, he still somehow managed to find himself on the wrong side of the law. As an avid fisherman, Saltis loved to take visiting colleagues on trips to the Winter Dam. Recent orders had been issued prohibiting fishing at the dam. Saltis, a life-long criminal whose list of offenses would shock even the most die-hard killer, simply scoffed at the new regulations. Rumors quickly spread that Saltis had threatened to shoot it out with the game wardens. On August 14, 1930, Saltis would get his chance. While fishing near the Winter Dam with visiting friends Ed Morrison and Joe Sedovich, Saltis was surprised by Warden Ernest Swift, who was accompanied by several other armed wardens. Somehow the men had stealthily snuck past Saltis' armed guards. The *Capitol Times* ran an account of the event as Saltis encountered the armed men. "'What's the idea with of all the artillery?' said Saltis, eyeing leveled rifles. 'I understand you want to shoot it out with me,' answered Swift, 'so here I am.'" As Saltis' guards moved in, a deadly shootout looked all but certain, yet Saltis sensed the futility of the situation and offered no resistance. Unlike his legal troubles in Chicago, he was merely fined $50 for fishing within 100 feet of a dam.

The *Oshkosh Daily Northwestern* carried the headline "Joe Saltis Fined." The paper stated that Saltis "pleaded guilty to charges of fishing within fifty feet of a dam." However this wasn't the first time Saltis had been caught illegally fishing at the dam. The *Capitol Times* reported that the conservation authorities had encountered Saltis fishing at the dam on several occasions. The paper reported, "About two weeks ago Warden Louis Oshesky reported that he found Saltis and several others casting at the dam. 'What are you doing here?' he asked. 'Waiting for Swift,' replied Saltis, and added, 'I understand he wants to take a swim.'"

When Prohibition ended in 1933, it brought with it financial

ruin for many of those whose fortunes were tied to bootlegging. At one point, what must have seemed like an endless supply of wealth completely dried up over night, leaving many in the business out in the cold. Saltis, like so many of his colleagues was hit hard by the effects, and soon found himself striving to stay afloat. Eventually Saltis ended up losing ownership of the property. In fact, Saltis' financial decline was so severe that when he died in 1947, he did so both poor and penniless. It goes without saying that Saltis was an interesting character who remains difficult to classify. Although he was denounced as a criminal thug by the newspapers, those who knew him reported that he was a kind and generous man willing to help out those less fortunate than him. We could debate the merits of Saltis' character indefinitely; however I believe that Saltis said it best when he appeared in court. The *Wisconsin State Journal* covered the trial when he said, "And another thing, people nicknamed me 'Polack' Joe Saltis. I'm not Polish, I'm a Czech. And I'm no gangster, I'm a country gentleman.'"

Tommy Gun Adventures:

You can spend the night in the historic Barker Lodge where you can rest in Northwoods luxury just like "Czech" Joe Saltis did, and be sure to ask David about Capone's sturgeon.

SHULLSBURG, WI

THE FIRST NATIONAL BANK
GETS ROBBED

TOWN TERRORIZED WHILE 5 ROBBERS WRECK BANK VAULT

Five Bandits Escape With Loot Estimated at $10,000 in Shullsburg, Wis.

The First National Bank Gets Robbed

Location:

The old bank is now the Water Street Place Historic Inn
202 W Water Street
Shullsburg, WI 53586
(608) 965-3228
www.WaterStreetPlace.com

Directions:

The restaurant and inn is located right on Water Street in downtown Shullsburg.

Gangster Lore:

No one is positive why certain banks were chosen to be robbed. Evidently gangsters did not discriminate when it came to stealing money. Robbed banks varied in nearly every type of demographic, and it didn't seem to matter as to the size of the bank, how much traffic it saw, what type it was, or even where it was located. As long as the establishment had money, it was susceptible to the gangsters. The rumor that the First National Bank was overflowing with the mining industries' payroll was exactly the type of thing that would put a bank on the outlaws must-rob list. Throw in the fact that the town did not possess a night watchman, and the bank moved directly to the top of the heap.

History:

1883 – Local businessman J.M. Brewster hired contractor Pete Richards to construct the two-story Italianate building. The building was initially set up to house several businesses.

1909 – The First National Bank joined several other businesses and began operation inside the building.

1925 – In the middle of the night, a gang of daring outlaws blew out the bank's vault, held the town hostage, and took off with the loot.

1930s – The Great Depression hit the First National Bank hard, and although the bank struggled to stay alive, it finally succumbed; it shuttered its doors and never re-opened.

1930s-1980 – Like most other historic buildings, the old bank saw the passing of numerous businesses through it doors. The building housed an assortment of attorneys, dentists, and miners. At one time the multi-use building functioned as a post office, city offices, and even as a library.

1981 – Unfortunately the building emptied of its businesses and the once booming structure sat empty as it slowly fell into disrepair. Over the years the building began to deteriorate as concerned citizens fought to save it.

1990 – The building, along with the Water Street Block, was added to the National Register of Historic Places.

2001 – Chuck and Jill Stabb purchased the building with dreams of restoring it back to its glory days. The married team began the process of transforming the run-down building into a beautiful restaurant, pub, and inn. Among the many improvements, Chuck added a historically accurate staircase leading to the upstairs level.

2002 – With the majority of the renovation completed, the Water Street Pub and Eatery officially opened.

2003 – With the restaurant and bar portion of the business in full bloom, the upstairs renovations were finally completed. With much excitement, the upstairs lodging was finished and the historic inn opened.

Currently – The historic restaurant and inn is open for business and lodging.

Source: Water Street Place

Investigation:

On June 23, 1925, the 1,200 residents of the small rural town of Shullsburg were awakened by a series of loud blasts echoing from the downtown. In a town that flourished from the mining industry, explosions were not deemed out of the ordinary and normally would not have aroused the suspicions of the sleeping townsfolk. What differentiated these explosions from the rest of the mining noise is that they rocked the town in the dead of the night. The explosions occurred at approximately 1am, when most of the town, even those who spent the night frolicking in the saloons, was sound asleep. Soon it became apparent that the blasts had originated from the First National Bank, as word quickly spread that the explosion was initiated by several gangsters who were robbing the place.

It was a well-known fact that Shullsburg did not employ a night patrolmen, a crucial error that left the town vulnerable to attack. From the start of their plans it was evident that the robbers were no mere amateurs. Before they even reached the sleeping town, the clever outlaws had stopped at the outskirts and cut the fire bell rope, three local telephone lines, severed two long distance circuits, and tore up a telegraph line—a trick that effectively isolated Shullsburg from the rest of the county and prevented any calls for help. After snipping the lines, the five bandits (Jack Adams, John Thompson, Jimmy Burns, and Frank Foster, and James (Joe) Dawsie) pulled their vehicle over just outside of town and stealthily made their way to the bank by foot. Three of the armed men remained outside to ward off any foolhardy attempts by the locals to disrupt their plans. The other two men forced their way in through the bank's heavy back door and immediately headed for the main vault. Once inside, the men set up their explosives on the bank vault and let loose. The *Oakland Tribune* wrote, "The first intimation of the robbery came when a heavy blast that wrecked the vault doors, shook the town, and awakened the citizens." The blast had attracted the attention of several miners who ventured down to the bank to see what all the commotion was. Again the *Oakland Tribune* wrote that the "miners who investigated were met with a fusillade of shots that drove them indoors." In a matter of minutes, the armed guards had taken complete control of the situation. The *Waterloo Daily Courier* wrote that "when the robbers were in command of the town two motorists drove into Shullsburg and were made the target of the robber guards, who shot tires of the car full of holes, threatened them and sent them fleeing on foot out of the town." Actually the vehicle was full of tourists, and according to the *Ironwood Daily Globe*, "A carload of South Dakota tourists, whose names were not learned, drove into town. One of the robber lookouts ordered the driver to stop, but he neglected to obey, with the result that the tires were shot off his machine and several bullets fired into the body of the car." The shooting aroused three men lodging at the Brewster Hotel, which was adjacent to the bank. The sleepy men looked out the windows, but withdrew their heads almost immediately as their curiosity almost got them killed when the gangsters sprayed bullets through the hotel's windows. Luckily, no one at the hotel was injured.

Inside the bank, the robbers were furiously trying to get the vault open. Over an hour had passed since the initial blast,  and after a series of failed attempts, the duo finally succeeded in breaking open the vault and they started scooping up all of the cash, gold, silver, and securities they could find. The gangsters had used nitroglycerine to blow the safe, which also caused extensive damage to the building. The *Freeport Journal-Standard* wrote that "the bank fixtures were practically ruined, the plate glass windows were blown out and other damage resulted aside from the fact that the vault doors and the interior of the vault itself were wrecked."

Outside the raging gunfight was in full motion. The fight was described by the newspapers as something right out of the old Wild West. Not content to just sit by and watch the bandits get away with the people's money, Louis O'Donnell, the town marshal, secretly headed up to the roof of a building across the street from the bank. The

Manitowoc Herald News reported that O'Donnell had been awakened by the blasts "and made a futile attempt to drive the bandits off. He fired at the two men stationed outside the bank, but was met with a fusillade of shots and had to seek shelter."

Once the robbers inside had taken everything they could get their hands on, they exited the bank and joined their colleagues as the gang strode down Water Street in single file to their high-powered car that was parked on the outskirts of town. The very first reports given to the media estimated the gang's take to be somewhere near $25,000. Later estimates placed the entire loss of everything that was taken closer to $500,000. Despite the devastatingly damaging robbery, the bank somehow re-opened the very next day. The *Freeport Journal-Standard* reported that bank officials "stated that the institution would continue doing business just as if nothing had happened."

Initially, the identities of the bandits were unknown. The *Freeport Journal-Standard* carried the speculation that the gangsters had previously scouted out the town writing, "Three strangers were seen in Shullsburg for several days preceding the robbery and it is the opinion of authorities there that they were advance agents for the bandit gang. One of the men was a peddler of shoes strings, another posed as an insurance agent, while the third claimed to be a miner. All three of the men disappeared the day before the robbery and have not been seen or heard of since." A few weeks after the robbery, a milk delivery man discovered many of the stolen documents on the side of the road in Illinois. The bag included mortgages, deeds, and life insurance policies, which were all extremely valuable papers that the gangsters had hastily overlooked.

In October of 1925, the bandits thought responsible for the Shullsburg bank robbery were apprehended. The group consisted of Jack Adams, John Thompson, Jimmy Burns, and Frank Foster, and James (Joe) Dawsie, who was better known as the notorious gangster "Chicago Blackie." The men were transported to Darlington, Wisconsin, and put on trial for the crime of bank robbery. On December 12, 1925, the jury came to a verdict on the charges and found Adams, Dawsie, and Thompson not guilty of the charges of complicity in the robbing the First National Bank. The other two men, Thomas and Foster, also had the cases against them thrown out of court.

The building that once housed the old bank is now is home to the Water Street Inn, which functions as a pub, restaurant, and inn. I was able to visit with the owners, whose love of the building is easily discernable right from the start. They told me that while doing renovations they discovered that the

second floor had originally been constructed with the sole purpose of providing lodging. This fact helped to convince Chuck and Jill that they should pay homage to the building's past and once again offer upstairs lodging. The building also contains several other unique features, including the fact that a creek once ran directly under the pub, and evidence of the old underground creek can still be seen today. The couple also found a wooden door that once lead to a tunnel under the street, leading to the old Opera House. Although the bank has been long gone from the building, its remnants are still visible all over the building, including the old solid brick walk-in bank vault that is prominently positioned directly behind the bar. This place truly keeps the history and feel of the past alive while providing you with the unique opportunity to spend the night in one of the luxurious rooms located right above the old bank. Don't worry—you can rest assured that when you spend the night at the inn you won't be woken up in the middle of the night by bank robbers trying to blow the safe.

Tommy Gun Adventures:

If you want to see more evidence of the bank robbery, head right down the road to the Badger Mine and Museum where they have tons of information of the robbery and even have the original bullet-ridden Brewster Hotel sign that the gangsters shot up.

Racine, WI

Dillinger Robs the
American Bank and Trust

EXTRA!

Kidnap Racine Banker
In Machine Gun Theft

RACINE, (AP)—Four robbers armed with machine guns today invaded the Racine downtown district, entered the American Bank and Trust company and escaped with an undetermined amount of cash, kidnaping the president of the bank, a woman clerk and a police officer.

Dillinger Robs the
American Bank and Trust

Location:
Racine Art Museum
(Formerly the American Bank and Trust Co.)
441 Main Street
Racine, WI 53401
(262) 638-8300

Directions: The old bank building is right in downtown
Racine near the civic center building. Take Main Street to
the north and once you pass Fifth Street the building will be
on your right.

Gangster Lore: In many circles John Dillinger was considered a folk hero for his exciting exploits of robbing banks.
During the Depression era, banks were rapidly foreclos-

ing on a substantial number of the loans they had issued. Almost overnight, property that had been passed down through generations of family farmers was being seized by the banking industry. Thousands of hard working families found themselves without their land, and throughout the country the banks were deemed as the corrupt culprits. It is ironic that in a time where gangsters operated without any concern for the law, it was the money hungry banks that were regarded as the true outlaws. This type of empathy allowed the gangsters to practically run amok in their pursuit of the banks' money. Whether warranted or not, many of the gangsters received Robin Hood like reputations. Everyday Americans secretly, and not so secretly, rooted for the gangsters to steal the money from the banks, which were responsible for stealing it from the people. Although public perception heavily favored the gangsters, not everybody was willing to easily depart with their money, especially the employees of the American Bank & Trust.

History:

1933 – The Dillinger gang robbed the American Bank and Trust.

2003 – The Racine Art Museum opened to the public.

Currently – The museum is open to the public.

Investigation:

For the people milling around Racine on November 20, 1933, the crisp-weathered afternoon would have appeared

like any other ordinary Wisconsin day. But for five gangsters, the day would be the culmination of a week's worth
of their diligent study and planning. The target was the
American Bank and Trust, which anchored Racine's thriv-
ing downtown district. In a perfect scenario, the men would
waltz into the bank and quickly clean out the vault with no
hassle or interference from the authorities. However, in the
world of bank robbing nothing is perfect, something the
outlaws would soon discover as they positioned their car
around the back side of the bank.

Although the exact identities of the men are officially unknown, it is widely believed that the gang consisted of John
Dillinger, Charles Makley, Russell Clark, Harry Pierpont,
and John Hamilton, all of which were skilled veterans of
crime. Clark eased their Illinois license plated car around
the back of the bank and found a spot on Fifth Street where
the idling car would not arouse unnecessary suspicion. It
was 2:30 in the afternoon when the four men quickly exited
the car and set off for the main entrance of the bank, leaving Clark as the get-away driver. Armed with sub-machine
guns, and extreme confidence, the men calmly entered
the bank and put their well devised plan into action. Right
from the start, their hopes for the perfect heist were foiled.
The *Racine Journal Times* wrote, "The foremost bandit,
a short chunky, fellow firing a round of shots at the floor.
These bullets struck the terraza floor and ricocheted in all
directions, one striking Harold Graham, a teller in the right

arm." Amongst all the whizzing lead the gang herded the frightened customers and employees into the back of the bank, where they were ordered to lay down on the floor, a move that was meant to stop outside onlookers from spotting the robbery.

The gangsters smoothly started to clean out the tellers' registers like the professionals they were, but the big money remained securely locked behind the main vault. Bank President Grover Weyland was dragged over and ordered at gunpoint to open the vault. A bit rattled, Weyland explained that he could not open the vault due to the fact that he only had half the combination. In an attempt to increase bank safety, a duel vault had been implemented which required the possession of two combinations that had been split between two employees. While the gangsters sought out the second portion of the code, L.C. Rowan, the assistant cashier, instead of lying down with the rest of the hostages, bravely darted off down the basement stairs and stomped hard on the alarm button. His action produced an immediate response, as the bank alarm loudly rang out.

While the ringing of the alarm had certainly caught the attention of the gangsters, it also alerted the Racine Police, whose headquarters were located only a few blocks away. The *Racine Journal Times* reported, "Sergts. Hanson and Worsley armed themselves. Hanson with a machine gun and Worsley with a revolver got into a machine with Officer Cyril Boyard and rushed to the bank building." The word "rushed" may not have been the most accurate description of their actions, as during this time period false alarms at banks were quite common, and over time they had helped to slow down the officers' response time. Once at the bank, Officer Boyard was the first one to enter and was immediately greeted by a loaded gun. In his book, *Public Enemies*, Bryan Burrough wrote that when Sergeant Hansen followed "his submachine gun pointed toward the floor. From the back of the bank Pierpont shouted, 'Get that cop with the machine gun.'" Makley did not hesitate and blasted off a round of bullets at Hansen who dropped to the floor. The officer had been stuck with two bullets, the first hit his body, and luckily the second merely grazed his forehead. The commotion was too much for a nearby lady who fainted at the sight of Hansen being hit. The robbery had rapidly unraveled, and sensing that the scene was approaching dangerous territory, the gangsters looked to escape as quickly as possible. Unfortunately the bank was not equipped with a back door, thus the men would have to fight their way out the front among the ever-expanding crowd of curious onlookers who had gathered outside.

To combat the possibility of enemy gunfire, the gangsters turned to the old standby of using hostages as human shields. The *Racine Journal Times* reported that the unlucky participants chosen for this task were Bank President Weyland, Officer Boyard, and Miss Ursula Patzke, who was a young clerk at the bank who pleaded with the gangsters asking, "'Do I have to go with you?' 'You bet you do,' answered the bandit." As he passed by the front windows Makley caught a glimpse of the growing crowd outside and, according to the *Racine Journal Times*, he picked up the police machine gun and said, "I'll show these people how we do things," and emptied the gun into the widows facing Fifth Street, shattering glass all over the outside. The *Sheboygan Press* covered the event writing, "A crowd of about 100 persons were outside the bank when the robbers emerged. Some fell flat on the sidewalk, others scattered in all directions when one of the bandits opened fire." Makley's actions dispersed the crowd long enough for the gangsters to parade their hostages outside, right by two additional officers who were sternly told to step aside.

With the hostages positioned along the car's running boards, the gangsters sped off south on Lake Avenue. They turned west on Seventh Street before being seen on West Sixth Street—heading off into the countryside of Wisconsin's farmland on their quest to reach the safety of Milwaukee. Along the way, the gangsters made sure to throw plenty of roofing tacks along the road to abruptly end any tailing from the police. Officer Boyard was the first of the hostages to be released when he was pushed off the running boards unharmed. With Boyard gone, the two remaining hostages were brought inside the vehicle to avoid detection. According to the *Ironwood Daily Globe*, the gangsters "seemed quite jovial during the 45 mile ride." The *Corsicana Daily Sun* reported, "Weyland said he and Mrs. Patzke were tied to trees and told to remain quiet for 15 minutes. He added that he had no difficulty freeing himself and his companion." Seemingly unaffected by the incident, and holding no apparent grudges, Weyland would later tell the newspapers that the boys were rather high class fellows.

Back at the bank, witnesses, bank employees, and law officers were swift in picking out police photos of the suspected robbers. The *Stevens Point Daily Journal* wrote, "Chief of Police Grover Lutter said he had obtained positive identifications of Dillinger, Charles Makley and Harry Pierpont as three of the bandits." Additional information was gathered, and soon the identities of the others were speculated on as the *Manitowoc Herald Times* wrote that "scores of persons saw some of the robbers and the chief said that several thought two of the robbers resembled Charles Makley and Russell Lee Clark, two reputed members of the Dillinger band." Being identified by the authorities meant little to the gangsters, as at this point in time they were all well-known wanted criminals whose fate had already been sealed. Although the robbery had not gone precisely as they had hoped, with none of them being killed or injured, it was still deemed a success. And even though they were unable to crack open the main vault, the men still netted over $5,000 per person—as the *Tipton Tribune* reported that "bank officials announced the loot amounted to about $28,000."

Today the old bank building is nearly unrecognizable from what it was like back in 1933. The Racine Art Museum has renovated the historic building into a modern space more fitting for the style of an art museum. However, all is not lost because the building does still contain the original bank vault from the 1930s. The bank vault is located in the basement of the museum and is normally not open to the general public, so be sure to freshen up your persuasion skills before visiting the museum.

Tommy Gun Adventures:

When you are done surveying the art museum, head down to the police headquarters building on 730 Center Street where they have a display of several pieces of memorabilia from the robbery, including one of Dillinger's machine guns. Warning—this is an operating police station, so those of you who are on the lam may want to avoid this adventure.

CASE #12

WOODRUFF, WI

MA BAILEY'S HOUSE OF ILL REPUTE

MARGARET BAILEY IS FINED $100 IN COURT

Charges Filed After Raid by Deputy Briggs; Game Violation is Alleged.

Margaret Bailey who operates a

Ma Bailey's House of Ill Repute

Location:

Ma Bailey's House

8591 Woodruff Rd.

Woodruff, WI 54568

Directions: Private Residence – Please View From Road

From downtown Woodruff head south on Highway 47.
Turn left on Co. Highway J and follow it for a bit, then turn
right on Fish Hatchery Road. Follow Fish Hatchery Road
until it forks on Woodruff Rd. Stay to the left and Ma's old
place will be the first house on your right. It is a yellow
house set back from the road.

Gangster Lore:

Whether you call it a cathouse, whorehouse, house of ill
repute, bawdy house, brothel, bordello, den of iniquity, or
den of vice, places of prostitution are viewed by us today
as shameful remnants of our wild and uncultured past.
Yet in this country you don't have to look back very far to

discover a time when "ladies of the night" were commonplace among the local establishments. The clientele of these places often included customers from every walk of life. On any given night you could spot powerful politicians mingling right alongside some of the nation's most wanted men. In fact, at Ma Bailey's place you may have had a difficult time separating the politicians from the gangsters.

History:

1903 – G.F. Sandborn purchased the rural secluded forest land.

1906 – After a couple years of logging the area, the land was purchased by the Home Investment Company for the price of $1,000. The land was then reclaimed by Oneida County.

1910— A homesteader named Louis Fredette was granted the land by the United States Government. Louis, along with his wife, struggled to make a life at their new home.

1912 – Woodruff resident Mr. John Burns purchased the property for $100.

1915 – Following in the path of former owners, Burns quickly gave up the hard life and sold the property to Andrew Gilquist for $300.

1917 – The property once again changed hands when Louis Bergevin coughed up $325 for the land.

1923 – Refreshed with new timber, the beautiful landscape was sold to Josie Kemist for $2,000.

1926 – Margaret Bailey (Ma Bailey) picked up the property for $10,000 and soon began operating the place as a brothel.

1943 – Ma Bailey paid a $400 fine for running a house of ill fame.

1944 – After suffering pressure from the IRS, Ma Bailey sold her place to Tom Otten and Becky Downs, who planned to operate the business as a restaurant and tavern.

1971 – Tom Otten passed away leaving the property to his estate.

1975 – The Otten family sold the property to Joe and Betty Kelly who called the place Joe Kelly's landing.

1989 – The Kelly family sold the establishment to John and Judy Allen of Chicago. Looking to pay homage to the place's history, the restaurant was re-named Ma Bailey's.

1996 – Ma Bailey's was sold to Guy Clark, who renamed the place Clark's Landing.

Currently – The place has been renovated into a family home; please view from the road.

Source: *The Lakeland Times*

Investigation:
Although Ma Bailey's original brothel has been shut down for over 70 years, its memory still holds an indelible repu-

tation throughout the area. Usually tracking down forgotten places is an arduous task filled with numerous difficulties. However, I was a bit surprised at the ease in which I was able to pin down the location Ma's old business. It seemed like everyone I spoke with knew of the place, yet when I asked for directions, I felt like I was being subjected to a visual examination, as though the person was about to divulge some deep dark hidden secret. Looking back on the situation, I guess it made sense that people might harbor some suspicion with someone poking around looking for a long closed brothel. Unfortunately, the place was unable to survive in its many incarnations as a bar and grill, and now is in the hands of private owners. But, back in the day…

Margaret "Ma" Bailey was described by the papers as a rather large woman who, like her husband, was always

smartly dressed. When asked, residents usually labeled her as a character. Although she looked like somebody's sweet grandmother, Ma Bailey was blessed at using obscene language to gain the attention of her clientele. Wishing to get a better idea of her appearance, I unsuccessfully tried to track down a photo of the illustrious entrepreneur. The local historical society told me that they had never even seen a photo of Ma, and they wondered if any were ever taken of her. In 1926, Ma purchased the property on Woodruff Road and opened up her house of ill fame. If Ma truly was a character of the Northwoods, then she certainly would have had a lot of company; during this time period the area was overflowing with all types of unique personalities including loggers, miners, woodsmen, and anyone else looking to escape the confines of city life, and of course no one sought out such refuge as much as the gangsters did. Ma's place afforded the gangsters the opportunity to rest and relax without the worry of being harassed by local authorities. Ma also had a solid reputation of running a fair and honest place of business, the irony being that her honest business was a cathouse and illegal speakeasy. The *Rhinelander Daily News* quoted a former handyman of Ma's as saying, "Ma was very strict, nobody got in unless Ma Bailey came to the door. And then she had to know you or a friend."

In 1943, Ma Bailey was forced to pay a $400 fine after being found guilty of running a house of ill fame. In addition to Ma being fined, two of her girls, Elise Rice and Gertrude Burke, were each fined $50 for the charge of soliciting prostitution. As a testament to Ma's popularity the *Rhinelander Daily News* quoted a long time resident as saying, "Nobody worries about Ma's

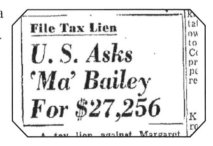

File Tax Lien

U. S. Asks 'Ma' Bailey For $27,256

place. She never bothers anybody and never caused trouble for this town. After all, this is a resort country." Yet, dealing with legal trouble was nothing new for Ma…with such widespread notoriety many wondered how she was even able to stay in business. Local historian Joyce Laabs wrote of a story for the local paper that may shed some light on how Ma continued operation. Laabs wrote that several young men were returning from Rhinelander when they got the urge to visit Ma's famed establishment for a quick beer. Although the place was nearly pitch black the men continued to venture in. As they walked in to the packed room they quickly saw that an x-rated movie was being shown. Their fear of being caught out there diminished as soon as the light went up and they noticed that the judge was the running the projector.

Selling the property and moving out of the Woodruff Road brothel did little to quell Ma's legal troubles. Once again the government looked to hit Ma with tax evasion charges, the same charges they brought against brothers Al and Ralph Capone. While Ma was fighting her charges down in Madison many in the Woodruff area came to her rescue. A 1951 article from the *Rhinelander Daily News* carried several endorsements in support of Ma Bailey. The article started off with this glowing assessment of Ma, and her trial:

> If Margaret 'Ma' Bailey has any enemies in Woodruff, they could not be heard Friday. In fact, it was easier to get an impression that 'old Ma Bailey' has 'a heart of gold.'

Only adding to the local legend of Ma's is the fact that the exact identities of the numerous gangsters who were said to have visited Ma's are not known. This was one of those places where people talked about all of the gangsters that hung out there, but perhaps out of fear, no specific names were ever mentioned. It is quite feasible that both Al Capone and his brother, Ralph, visited the place at least once. Al had a hideout in the woods of Couderay, WI, and Ralph lived right down the road in Mercer. The legend is that gangsters who were in the area spent the early part of their evening drinking and gambling in the speakeasies of Mercer and Minocqua. After a few hours of illegal fun they would then drive out to Ma's either to spend their newfound winnings, or to seek comfort from their losses. It is also quite possible that Dillinger and his gang made an appearance at the brothel. Dillinger colleague John Hamilton had some relatives up in the UP of Michigan, and the gang most likely would have traveled through the area before their big shoot-out in Manitowish Waters, WI. However, it is more probable that the majority of gangsters who hung out at Ma's were less well known than the previously mentioned men, which I feel only enhances the intrigue around the history of Ma's, being that you never really knew just exactly who you might run into. Of course, this is all merely speculation as unfortunately— or maybe fortunately—Ma Bailey took the names of her friends and customers to the grave with her.

North Leeds, WI

Baby Face Nelson
Crashes into North Leeds

Baby Face Nelson
Crashes into North Leeds

Location:

North Leeds Grocery Store – Now Thirsty's Bar and Grill
Crossroads of Highway 22 and Highway 60
North Leeds, WI
(608) 635-8990

Directions:

From South Leeds head north on US 51 until you see Highway 22 veering off to the right. Take 22 for a short distance until it crosses Highway 60. This is the intersection where Baby Face Nelson crashed. You will see Thirsty's Bar and Grill on your left side. This was the old grocery store that Nelson and his wife entered to make a phone call.

Gangster Lore:

For gangsters on the lam travel was often an extremely stressful experience. Every new place they visited posed the danger of being discovered by the general public and authorities. Yet at the same time, the gangsters hardly ever dressed down in order to blend in with the local residents. It would seem unlikely that such obsessively observant men would simply overlook such an identifying detail. Perhaps they were truly confident that their ability to outsmart the authorities would override their apparent need to always appear dapper. While traveling up to Little Bohemia, Baby Face Nelson and Tommy Carroll would both need to utilize all of their survival techniques in order to blend in with the town folk, even though the two gangsters were dressed to the nines.

History:

Early 1900s – The small general store was called the "North Leeds Store" and was operated by the Dieruf family.

1900s – George Kampman ran the store and began having a Friday night fish fry.

1934 – Baby Face Nelson crashed his car at the crossroads and entered the store to use the payphone.

1940s – The grocery store was run by Arnold Zelmer.

1995 – The store was purchased by Ray Tyrich, who turned the grocery business into a bar and grill called the Homestead Bar and Grill.

2009 – Tammy Dickerson and Don Piffl purchased the bar and grill and renamed it Thirsty's.

Currently – The building houses Thirsty's Bar and Grill.

Investigation:

On April 20, 1934, Baby Face Nelson along and his wife, Helen, were traveling north up to Little Bohemia. Following close behind in another vehicle were Tommy Carroll and his girlfriend Jean Delaney. The outlaw group was looking to meet up with John Dillinger and the rest of the gang for some much needed relaxation in Wisconsin's Northwoods. Early on, the road trip had been pretty uneventful, but things quickly changed when the group hit the small town of North Leeds. While passing through the crossroads where US 51 intersected with Wisconsin roads 44 and 60, Nelson crashed into a canning truck driven by local employee John Delany (often referred to as Jack Delany by other researchers). Luckily no one was injured during the crash, and Nelson and Delany hopped out of their respective vehicles in order to assess the damage. Eager to keep the police out of the equation, many researchers contend that Nelson simply paid Delany off right there on the spot, and then continued on his way up to Little Bohemia. However, the locals of the time told a much different and intriguing story of what really happened.

During my research trip to North Leeds, residents kept telling me that I definitely had to speak with a man named Bill Hahn, who as a life-long resident of nearby Arlington was said to have first-hand knowledge of the Baby Face incident. This really caught my attention because finding someone with a first- hand account of the gangsters is

extremely rare. Over the years I had spoken with numerous people who have shared with me their family's encounter with gangsters, but these were often second and third-hand reports. I had never been able to personally hear a story about the gangsters from someone who was there. Needless to say, I was hell bent on finding Bill Hahn. Now, in a small town like Arlington you would think that finding someone would be a short and simple process. However, after discovering that Bill was not at his home, I spent the better part of a full day tracking him down. After barely missing him at several of his favorite haunts, I arrived at the Arlington Curling Club only to find that I was once again 10 minutes too late. I finally met up with Bill in a small bar located approximately 20 miles outside of town. Taking a reluctant break from a serious looking game of Euchre, Bill recounted the story of what he witnessed back in 1934. As an 11-year-old boy, Bill was sitting next to the bread box outside the grocery store waiting for some school friends when he noticed a black car coming over from the east. As the car quickly approached the crossroads, it crashed into the truck of John Delany. Bill said that both Nelson and Helen got out of their car and headed into the store, where Bill could see Nelson making a phone call. While Nelson was inside the store, Bill witnessed another large black car pull over and wait about 100 yards away. Although he remembered that it was a large fancy car, Bill was unable to see who occupied the vehicle (Carroll and Delaney) because the car's dark windows were obscuring his view. Not knowing that the strangers were some of the most wanted men in America, the accident elicited little excitement from Bill. Even though Bill was in fifth grade at the time he can still recall the details of how well Nelson and his wife were dressed. After placing his call, Nelson quickly exited the grocery store and spoke a few words to Delany before walking back to his vehicle. The whole event only lasted a couple minutes before the three cars took off toward the Arlington Garage in Arlington. Once the commotion of the accident had ceased, Bill continued on with his day and gave the event no special thought. Several days later the town was buzzing from the news of the deadly shootout that had taken place up at Little Bohemia. As the gangsters pictures were plastered all over the newspapers, town residents were able to identify Baby Face Nelson as the man who had crashed his car.

Amazingly, Bill told me that throughout the last 75 years not one media outlet had sought him out to record his story. In fact, before I spoke with him the only other

Reveal Nelson In Accident At Portage

group that had even remotely showed interested in his story was the Poynette Historical Society. After hearing this I felt a bit better knowing that Bill's first hand story would live on long after his Euchre game had ended.

Tommy Gun Adventures:

You can still sit out front of Thirsty's Bar and Grill and watch the crossroads in the same spot where the young Bill Hahn witnessed the crash in 1934. You can also pop into Thirsty's to see where Baby Face and Helen made their telephone call. While you are there, you may want to order some food before heading off to Bell Ford in Arlington.

Arlington, WI

Baby Face Nelson
Controls His Infamous Temper

Baby Face Nelson
Controls His Infamous Temper

Location:

Arlington Garage – Now Bell Ford

209 Main Street

Arlington, WI 53911

(608) 635-4383

www.bellfordinc.net

Directions:

Bell Ford (Arlington Garage) is located on Main Street in Arlington.

Gagster Lore:

When it came to Baby Face Nelson, it was a virtual toss up as to what version of him you would encounter. On one hand, Baby Face was a polite, jovial, and extremely well-mannered young man. Many who knew Baby Face described him as a very likable person, which would account for the undying trust and loyalty he garnered from his closest friends and family members. However, you may want to postpone nominating Baby Face for a Good Samaritan award, as he also was a stone cold killer who loved to shoot up towns while spewing out obscenity-laced orders. This erratic behavior forced even some of his colleagues to second guess their association with him. Of course, the mass media likes to portray Baby Face as a one dimensional psychopath who was hell bent on killing as many people as he could. Yet, as you will discover throughout this book, when the pressure was the highest, Baby Face performed at his best.

History:

1900s – Local residents William F. Bell, Ed Gundlach, John Stevenson and A.C. Ellickson started the first garage in Arlington aptly named the Arlington Garage.

1918 – With the rapidly rising success of the automobile, the owners decided that their business needed a new home, and the garage was moved across the street to its current location.

1931- The automobile garage became a Ford dealership.

1934 – Suffering from a nearby accident, Baby Face Nelson drove his damaged car to the Arlington shop to have some repair work done.

1949 – Gene Bell took over the family business. Bell greatly expanded the building by adding a new large showroom to properly display his vehicles. Several additional repair areas were also included in the expansion.

1962 – William Bell became a partner in Bell Motors.

1985- Bill Bell took ownership of the dealership from his father, Gene Bell.

Currently – Bell Ford is open to the public.

Investigation:

Tensions must have ran high when Baby Face crashed his car into a canning employee's truck while on his way up north. As one of the most wanted men in America it was essential to Nelson that things moved quickly, and quietly, as to avoid detection. While most crime scholars believe that Nelson hurriedly paid off Delany and continued on with his trip, the real story involved the two men agreeing that the vehicles would be brought to the Arlington Garage (Bell Ford) to have the service work completed. In her book *Arlington, Wisconsin: The First 100 Years,* Geraldine Rouse wrote about the incident:

> A collision of a canning company car and an Illinois vehicle necessitated the cars being brought to Bell Motors for repairs. As was customary when an accident had occurred, a crowd gathered to observe the damage. The Illinois car was a fancy one for those times, with heavy tires and laminated windows. Its damage was mostly a crumpled fender which

rubbed on the wheel. Estimates were made and the two drivers went to the factory to settle up. The Illinois driver readily paid cash and he and his woman companion were soon on their way.

Rouse also included the story where witnesses later reported that for the entire time Nelson was inside the garage he was positioned in a manner that his back was up against the wall, thus preventing anyone from sneaking up behind him. Just in case a fast getaway became necessary, fellow gangster Tommy Carroll had left his car running across the street outside of Heideman's Tavern while he slipped inside for a few drinks. While Baby Face was occupied inside the garage, witnesses reported that Helen waited patiently in their car. Rouse wrote that local resident Jessie Stevenson had spotted Helen sitting in the car, and feeling sympathy for the woman, Jessie walked across the street and politely invited Helen over to her house for a bite to eat while she waited. Helen, a veteran of the gangster lifestyle, kindly declined. A few minutes later, Nelson's car was fixed and the couple hurriedly sped off north on Highway 51. The *Stevens Point Journal* reported that "Nelson paid Delaney $280, more than the amount of the damages." The *Journal* went on to report that Delaney "identified Nelson as the driver of the automobile which collided with his machine near North Leeds." Delaney was also able to finger Tommy Carroll as the driver of the other vehicle. Once the town had learned about the identity of the traveling motorists they speculated that Helen had refused Jessie's offer of food in order to stay close to the car, which was thought to be loaded with weapons and ammunition.

Tommy Gun Adventures:
You can re-trace the steps of Baby Face Nelson as you pull up to Bell Ford. Once inside be sure to keep your back against the wall. When you are done browsing around you can hop back in your car and head off up Highway 51 toward Portage just like Nelson and Carroll did.

ARLINGTON, WI

TOMMY CARROLL GRABS A DRINK

116

Tommy Carroll
Grabs a Drink

Location:
Arlington Inn
(Formerly
Heideman's Tavern)
226 Main Street
Arlington, WI 53911-8500
(608) 635-4963

Directions:
The Arlington Inn is located
on Main Street in Arlington.

Gangster Lore:
Although not as well known today as some of his contemporaries, Tommy Carroll spent much of his criminal career causing chaos with infamous outlaws like John Dillinger and Baby Face Nelson. Carroll was a close associate to both men and heavily participated in many of their exploits, yet for some unknown reason the national notoriety that erupted around his colleagues always seemed to elude Carroll, as evidenced by the fact that the people of Arlington don't ever remember his 1934 visit.

History:
1878 – The actual building may have existed much earlier than 1878, but the first recorded record of it came when

117

Jack McMillan paid a $25 fee to operate his hotel on the property.

1886 – McMillan and Dick Hartley paid $100 to obtain a license to operate a saloon.

1897 – The hotel and saloon was purchased by Mr. A. J. Lake. Mr. Lake then moved the saloon next door from the hotel.

1900-1905 – Albert Bruns acquired and operated the saloon and hotel.

1905-1920 – Like so many other taverns records show that the business passed through several proprietors during this time period including R. Stiemke, Louis Haupt, Adolph Graack, F.W. Kleinert, and W.B. Schmidt.

1920-1933 – During Prohibition the tavern was officially closed down. The Haupt family operated the building as a general store.

1933 – Once Prohibition ended, and the liquor could once again flow, Al Heideman purchased the building. Heideman had grand plans for the building and soon renovated the store back into a tavern. Heideman also expanded the building by adding a pool room and barber shop.

1934 – While waiting for Baby Face Nelson to finish his business over at the Arlington Garage (Now Bell Ford), Tommy Carroll entered the bar and tossed back a couple drinks to calm his nerves.

1938 – Howard Dobratz took over ownership of the business.

1950- 2001 – Keeping with its tradition of frequently
changing ownership the business was operated by Lloyd
Mathes, Gordan Hustad, Dale King, and Mark Olsen.

2001 – The bar was purchased by Casey Tomlinson.

Currently – The bar is open to the public.

Investigation:
After the car accident in North Leeds, Tommy Carroll and
his girlfriend, Jean Delaney, tried to discretely follow Baby
Face Nelson to the Arlington Garage. It appears that Carroll
was more adept at robbing banks than he was at subterfuge,
as several residents reported seeing an unknown car with
Illinois plates stationed outside of Heideman's Tavern with
its engine running. While Baby Face was dealing with the
consequences of the crash up, Carroll walked into Heideman's Tavern and downed a few beers in order to calm his
frayed nerves. Little is known about what transpired while
Carroll was inside. Whatever conversation was exchanged
inside the bar has been lost to history. It is engrossing to
speculate on what occurred inside Heideman's Tavern. Did
any of the locals ask Carroll any questions? Was the tavern
extremely busy or completely quiet? How close of an eye
did Carroll keep on the garage? All of these questions, and
a myriad of others, make the 1934 encounter so fascinating.

When I visited Heideman's Tavern, now called the Arlington Inn, I was excited at the prospect of someone shedding  some light on the events of 1934. My excitement quickly dissipated when I found that the current owners and employees were completely unfamiliar with the history their bar played in Wisconsin's gangster past. In an all too familiar situation, I found myself trying to explain the importance that Tommy Carroll and Baby Face Nelson had in 1934, while receiving ambivalent responses from the polite staff. In retrospect, I thought that perhaps the fact that no one remembered Tommy Carroll's actions inside Heideman's Tavern proved that he was exceedingly better at blending in than I had originally thought.

Tommy Gun Adventures:

The Arlington Inn is still open for business and you can wander in and grab yourself a beer just like Tommy Carroll did. You may want to enjoy your drink up by the front window where you can easily keep a vigilant eye on Bell Ford (Arlington Garage) across the street.

PORTAGE, WI

BABY FACE NELSON
DITCHES HIS CAR

Baby Face Ditches His Car

Location:

Discount Liquor (Formerly A.R. Slinger's Garage)

211 East Wisconsin Street, Portage, WI

(608) 742-6226

Directions:

The building is located in downtown Portage on East Wisconsin Street (Hwy 51).

Gangster Lore:

For the gangsters of the early 1900s, lax regulations and endless amounts of money made for an explosive combination. Long before credit checks and multiple forms of identification, you could easily secure items with nothing more than cash and a credible alias. The gangsters of the time were grand masters at manipulation and subterfuge, and it was not uncommon for them to utilize dozens of different aliases. It was extremely rare, if at all, that the men would register motel rooms, cars, and even marriage licenses under their legal names. While they were on the lam, possessions meant relatively little the fleeing outlaws. With cash being able to sort out even the most complicated messes, most of the men religiously wore a money belt around their waist to ensure that if fleeing was deemed necessary, they would also have their most important weapon. Time and time again the gangsters were forced to leave behind their goods, including their wives and girlfriends, at the drop of a hat in order to make a clean getaway. Considering what waited ahead for Baby Face, he should have counted himself luckily that is was only his car that was lost in Portage.

History:

1929- The Portage City Directory listed the Slinger Foundry Machine & Auto Co. at 211-215 E. Wisconsin St. Andrew R. (A.R.) Slinger was listed as the acting president of the company.

1934- Baby Face Nelson left his damaged car at Slinger's Garage with the assurance that one of his business colleagues would be by to pick it up.

1940s- Changing ownership throughout the years, the building operated as Hyland Garage Company.

1950s-1970s- The business remained a car dealership and operated as Hill Chevrolet.

1970s-2000- Several different liquor stores, including Havey's Liquor operated in the south end of the building.

Eventually the liquor store was renamed Discount Liquor.

2002- Current owner, Kevin Mathieus, purchased the Discount Liquor business.

Currently- The old garage now houses Discount Liquor, and is open to the public.

Investigation:

Fresh off of his car crash in North Leeds, Baby Face Nelson and his wife, Helen, drove up Highway 51 on their way to Little Bohemia. Following close behind in another car was Tommy Carroll, and his girlfriend, Jean Delaney. Bad luck seemed to have plagued the fated trip from the start, and things only got worse when the makeshift repairs Nelson's car had received in Arlington quickly failed him. As he sputtered into Portage, Nelson's car became a liability, knowing that another breakdown would again attract unwanted attention, he desperately sought out a garage to ditch the clunker. The bad luck that had been looming over the trip momentarily cleared, because as soon as Nelson reached Portage he spotted Slinger's Garage positioned directly off of Hwy 51. The garage was owned and operated by Andrew R. (A.R.) Slinger, who attended the needs of his new customer. Nelson told Slinger that he was interested in storing his car for a few days. The *Ironwood Daily Globe* wrote that Nelson slyly stated "someone else will call for it in a couple of days." After several days had passed, and no one had shown up for the car, Slinger began to get a bit suspicious, and rather than take any chances, he decided to notify the Department of Justice. Slinger's mistrust in the situation may seem a little overboard today, but this was in the middle of the gangster fever that swept America where everybody was on the lookout for irregular behavior. Each and every day the authorities received hundreds of alleged sightings of wanted gangsters, these questionable reports often put the outlaws in dozens of places at once. The odds that the Feds would uncover the owner of the abandoned car seemed highly unlikely, as Nelson was a grizzled veteran of the criminal lifestyle who used a mind-boggling number of aliases. It wasn't until the Feds captured Nelson's wife, Helen Gillis, after the shootout at Little Bohemia that the pieces began to fall into place. When the authorities were rummaging through Helen's purse they discovered a claim check for the abandoned vehicle leading them to Slinger's Garage. Once the authorities acquired the claim, they were able to trace the car back to Nelson, and were then able to re-trace the car back to the crash at North Leeds.

I found myself back on the trail of Baby Face and I had just left the original site of his accident, when I followed the highway up north until Portage, where my mission was to locate the old Slinger's Garage. The problem with so many of these gangster cases is that nobody recalls where these old businesses were. Most people have a hard time remembering businesses that closed twenty years ago, much less one that closed eighty years ago. However, over the years I have learned that sometimes when standard research fails, common sense is often the great equalizer, and that is actually what saved me in Portage. Looking through old city directories I discovered that Andrew Slinger had several different addresses listed, depending on what year I consulted. His business seemed to change places from year to year, and to make matter worse the 1934 city directory was missing from the archives leaving his address at the time of Baby Face unknown. I spoke with several librarians, newspaper reporters, and long time residents of Portage, none of whom could tell me where Slinger's Garage once stood. This was the point where common sense finally intervened on my behalf. I assumed that if Nelson drove up on 51 from the south with a dying car, he most likely would have wanted to stop at the first garage that he encountered. I further assumed that in order to avoid unnecessary travel, the garage would have had to been within eyesight of 51. With this I started my search on the south end of town and slowly walked north along 51 looking for buildings that could have housed a garage at some point in time. Realizing that perhaps over the years the building had been remolded, or even torn down, I did not hold out any hope of easily finding it. My outlook quickly changed when I passed by an old brick building that vaguely resembled a long lost garage. Everything about the building seemed right, it was on the south end of town, it was positioned directly on 51, and to top it all off, it was now a business that the gangsters would certainly approval of. With my excitement level peaking, I hurriedly walked in to Discount Liquors.

Walking inside the store I was greeted by the owner of the business, Kevin Mathieus, who immediately smiled when I brought up Baby Face Nelson. Mathieus confirmed that his

store was indeed the old garage where Nelson dumped off his old car. This encounter was a fresh change of pace to my normal endeavors where my inquiries into the

history of a location are almost always met with bewilderment. The first things Mathieus pointed out to me were the large showroom windows which during the 1930s would have showcased the flashy new cars on display. The overall space inside the old showroom is much smaller than you would imagine, especially when compared to today's huge dealerships. Mathieus pointed out that at the time only a few cars would have been able to fit into the cramped showroom. The unique aspect of the place is that outside of not being a car dealership, the building has really not changed all that much over the years. Even the back office area where deals were struck and the paper work was sorted out remained much like it was during the 1930s. Mathieus, like everyone else, has no idea what became of Baby Face's run down car, and although the car is no longer there, the unique history of the place still is.

Tommy Gun Adventures:

Follow in Nelson and Carroll's footsteps as you exit the store continue north on Highway 51 and make your way up to Little Bohemia.

MANITOWISH WATERS, WI

THE FEDS PLAN THEIR ATTACK

The Feds Plan Their Attack

Location:

Voss' Birchwood Lodge

311 Voss Rd – US Hwy 51

Manitowish Waters, WI 54545

(715) 543-8441   www.vossbl.com

Directions:

From downtown Manitowish Waters head south on US
Highway 51. The resort is just a few miles outside of town
on the left side of the road.

Gangster Lore:

The Northwoods are overflowing with legend and lore. For
the most part, people living in the region subscribe to the
'live and let live' lifestyle. Since the early days this type of
laissez-faire outlook has acted like a strong beacon draw-
ing in all manner of unique individuals looking to live life
in their own fashion. The Northwoods philosophy dictated

that as long as a person wasn't hurting anyone, they should be left alone to do as they please. While vacationing in Manitowish Waters, the gangsters were banking on this liberal philosophy for their survival…it is just too bad no one mentioned this to Voss' Birchwood Lodge.

History:

1908 – Brothers Henry and Edward Voss purchased 100 acres of land on Spider Lake.

1910 – Henry and his new wife, Ruth LaPorte, began construction of a home on Henry's land. The couple set out to transform their property into a Northwoods retreat.

1924 – The main lodge was built which provided 17 additional rooms. The addition also included a dance hall and bar, providing vacationers a place to gather and socialize.

1928 – Another structure was constructed near the road that functioned as a coffee shop and garage.

1934 – With the Dillinger gang staying at nearby Little Bohemia, the Feds met at Voss' resort to map out their plan of attack.

1958 – The Voss children, Audrey and Lloyd took over the family business. The resort's marina was added as well.

1965 – The resort underwent an extensive renovation and the rooms of the main lodge were expanded in size and decreased in number.

2006 – After the death of Audrey, her daughter and grandson took over the reins of the family resort.

Currently – The resort is open to the public.

Investigation:

Henry and Ruth Voss routinely traveled down the road from their lodge on Highway 51 to pop in and visit Ruth's sister, Nan Wanatka, who along with her husband, Emil, owned the nearby Little Bohemia Lodge. Normally at these visits the couples would simply shoot the breeze with one another as they combed over the local gossip. But during April of 1934, Nan would have no time for idle chit chat, as she found herself desperately searching for a way to alert the authorities to the fact that the most wanted men in America were holed up at her lodge. Her solution would involve Henry Voss and ultimately put his resort right smack in the middle of the nation's most important manhunt.

Once Nan's plan was hatched (see Little Bohemia) a letter was smuggled out to Henry Voss, who quickly headed off to the nearest secure phone in Rhinelander. Once he arrived in Rhinelander, Henry placed a call to the authorities. His call was returned by Melvin Purvis who, based on the credibility of the tip, chartered a plane, gathered his agents, and headed for Wisconsin. With Dillinger and his gang not scheduled to depart from Little Bohemia until the following morning, the Feds firmly believed that there was plenty of time to formulate a full-proof plan of capturing the fugitives. However, when Purvis and his men landed in Rhinelander they received the heart-breaking news that Dillinger and his men had changed their plans, and were now poised to leave the lodge at any minute. Racing from Rhinelander, Purvis and his men arrived at Voss' place shortly before 9pm. With no time to spare, the agents scrambled to devise a plan to capture the most elusive men in America all while sprawled out in Voss' parking lot. Within a few minutes the caravan of Federal Agents stealthily pulled out of Voss' driveway and headed up toward Little Bohemia, fatefully unaware of the misfortune that awaited them.

Adding even more infamy to the lodge is the fact that right outside along Highway 51 was the area in which George "Baby Face" Nelson let the Feds have it (see Shootout at Little Bohemia).

Tommy Gun Adventures:
From the parking lot of Voss' Lodge you can re-trace the footsteps of the agents as you put together your own plan to race off north on Highway 51 to Little Bohemia.

MANITOWISH WATERS, WI

SHOOTOUT AT LITTLE BOHEMIA

The Shootout at Little Bohemia

Location:

Little Bohemia Lodge

142 Highway 51 S

Manitowish Waters, WI 54545

(715) 543-8433

Directions:

Little Bohemia is located on Highway 51 in Manitowish Waters, just north of Voss' Birchwood Resort.

Gangster Lore:

In 1934, outlaw John Dillinger was considered Public Enemy #1 by the U.S. Government. Dillinger's series of bank robberies, shootouts, and daring escapes had captured the imagination of a general public that was battered by the Great Depression. Many secretly—and not so secretly—envied the bank-robbing desperado. Many of those who heard of Dillinger's exploits felt he was simply acting out their inner desires. The banks of the time were widely viewed as soulless money hungry institutions that were hell bent of taking people's land. This perception inevitably led to the classic good vs. evil scenario in which Dillinger came out looking like the folk hero. When Dillinger's wanted photo was flashed across theater screens before the start of a movie, crowds widely cheered for him. He quickly became the biggest celebrity of his time. Regardless of how he was perceived, every time Dillinger showed up in Wisconsin, trouble wasn't far behind; his visit to Little Bohemia would be no different.

History:

1931 – Emil Wanatka grew tired of the dangers of the Chicago lifestyle and desired to move his family up to the tranquility of Wisconsin's Northwoods. Emil fell in love with a gorgeous piece of land near Little Star Lake and de-cided to purchase it. Wanatka had the grand plan of turning his newly acquired land into a resort lodge.

1934 – The deadly shoot out occurred at the lodge after the authorities were tipped off to the fact the nation's most wanted men were staying at Little Bohemia.

2006 – Dan and Debbie Johns purchased the place.

2008 – The movie *Public Enemies* was partly filmed on location at Little Bohemia. The lodge was transformed to look much like it did back in 1934.

Currently – Little Bohemia restaurant is open to the public.

Investigation:

Of all Wisconsin's gangster hot spots, Little Bohemia is by far the most infamous. Thanks in part to the 2009 film *Public Enemies*, Little Bohemia has seen a drastic increase in popularity. For those of you that caught the period picture, forget the overdone Hollywood version of events, because this is what really happened. It was the offseason of 1934, which meant that the resort town was completely dead—it wasn't filled with Chicago tourists like it is today. Nestled among the thick woods of the north sat the Little Bohemia Resort. The lodge was constructed by former Illinois resident Emil Wanatka, who invested his life savings into his dream of running the resort. Originally from Illinois, Wanatka had moved to the Northwoods to escape the big city dangers of Chicago. Ironically, it was Wanatka's past underworld connections that would end up bringing the Chicago gangsters to the Northwoods.

On the afternoon of April 20, Wanatka was working the bar when Homer Van Meter, his girlfriend Mickey Conforti, and Pat Reilly walked through the front door. Posed as vacationers, Van Meter and his companions sat down for

THIS IS WHERE GUNMEN ELUDED FEDERAL MEN'S 'TRAP'

lunch before inquiring about the possibility of renting the place. Van Meter explained that a few of his buddies would be arriving later that evening

137

and were in need of a place to stay. The real reason behind Van Meter's visit had more to do with safety than simply securing reservations. Van Meter had been sent ahead to scope out the place and to ensure that the coast was clear for the rest of the gang to arrive. The idea that Wanatka had prior knowledge that the gangsters were coming is a contention that is still hotly debated. Whether he expected the men or not didn't seem to matter, and Wanatka showered them with hospitality. The newly checked-in guests were shown to their rooms. The first indication that something was not right occurred when two lodge employees carried the guests' luggage up to the quarters. When the luggage was retrieved, the staff commented on how heavy the bags were and assumed that the men must have been salesmen of some type. The staff thought nothing more of it and went about their normal routines. Little did they know that the bags' weight came from the virtual armory that the gangsters traveled with. Within a couple of hours the rest of the gang had arrived safely at the lodge. Without any doubt the group that was now assembled was the all-star list of 1930s gangsters. Never had so many big names (and egos) gathered under one roof. In one fell swoop the FBI could check off nearly all the names from their Most Wanted list. The list of menacing figures, and their molls at Little Bohemia was:

John Dillinger
Homer Van Meter and his girlfriend Mickey Conforti

Baby Face Nelson and his wife Helen Gillis

Tommy Carroll and his girlfriend Jean Delaney
John "Red" Hamilton and his girlfriend Pat Cherrington
Pat Reilly

All the excitement and action was a refreshing change of pace to Wanatka, whose business had been suffering for quite some time. Upon arrival, Baby Face provided Wanatka with a letter of introduction from a Chicago acquaintance of Wanatka's named Louie Cernocky. Nelson believed that the letter would put the group in good graces with their host, yet Bryan Burrough wrote in his book, *Public Enemies*, that Wanatka "wasn't stupid. He saw how Nelson ripped up the introductory note from Cernocky after letting him read it." This suspicion would be the beginning of a long list of things about the group that didn't quite add up. The rest of the night was mostly uneventful. Several of the men gathered around to play some poker, even enticing Wanatka to play a hand or two before he bowed out due to the high stakes the men were playing for. Days later Wanatka opened up about Dillinger and the card game, telling the *Salt Lake Tribune*, "I played cards every day. Say, he had a roll of money big enough to choke a cow." As the night wore on, Wanatka began to notice other little details that also seemed out of place for the vacationing group. First, all of the men were smartly dressed in extremely expensive suits, especially in the heart of the Great Depression. Wanatka and his wife, Nan, also noticed that all the men seemed to have a large lump on the sides of the jackets. Later in the evening, Wanatka spotted that the lumps were actually guns as he caught a glance of the pistol hanging from Dillinger's side. With heightened senses, the hosts quietly watched for any further signs of trouble. It is believed that Wanatka's suspicions were confirmed when he noticed several photos of Dillinger sprawled out on the newspaper's front pages. Yet, Wanatka himself seemed to contradict this version of events when he told all the newspapers, including the *Ironwood Daily Globe,* "'sure I knew it was Dillinger.'" "'Those Chicago cops couldn't find him, and in Indiana they couldn't hold him, so why should I have tried to take him.'" Knowing that the most dangerous men in the country were camped out in their home must have posed a troublesome affair for the Wanatka family. If any sleep was to come, it would not be from the gangsters. All night long the gang kept constant patrol of the lodge, their footsteps and hushed whispering continued on through the wee hours of the night.

The next morning, the nerve-rattled Wanatka awoke to discover that Tommy Carroll had beaten him to the daylight. Carroll inquired about some breakfast for the gang and retreated back upstairs. It is alleged that later that morning Wanatka ushered Dillinger aside and confronted him about

his true identity. Legend states that Dillinger, ever the gentleman, assured Wanatka that no trouble would be caused and that the gang simply wanted a peaceful place to rest and regroup for a few days. Dillinger then smoothed over the situation even more with the promise that the gang would pay generously for the hospitality. With Wanatka desperate for money, this assurance helped ease the stress that accompanied housing such deadly lodgers. The rest of the day was filled with Wanatka joining the gang in a round of target shooting, a foreshadowing of the gun battle that was brewing on the horizon. Perhaps the story that is most often told of Little Bohemia involves a game of catch that took place between Baby Face and eight-year-old Emil junior What started out as a fun way to pass the time ended painfully when Emil Jr. quit, complaining that the ever volatile Nelson was chucking the ball way too hard.

'Kept My Mouth Shut So Dillinger Wouldn't Hurt Me,' Says Resort Owner

With the men preoccupied with their games, the women offered their assistance with the cooking and cleaning, while Mrs. Wanatka headed off to a birthday party. Before getting to the party, Mrs. Wanatka shipped off a letter to the District Attorney in Chicago, alerting them to Dillinger's presence in Wisconsin. While at the party, Nan couldn't help but to open up about her dangerous house guests. Inside of merely venting about her worries, Mrs. Wanatka and her family devised a plan to call the FBI's Chicago office. Needing to discuss the plan with her husband, Nan requested that her brother-in-law stop at the lodge and find out if was okay for him to contact the authorities. It was decided that a message would be snuck out of the lodge hidden in a pack of cigarettes signaling the go ahead for a call to be placed to the authorities. The next morning when the brother-in-law stopped by, he was handed the cigarettes with the stowed away message. Inside, the note confirmed that the plan to notify the authorities should proceed. It was obvious that all those involved in the plan knew of its danger. If any of the gangsters found out they were being snitched on, the retribution would have been deadly. During this time all of the phones in the area were party lines, meaning that anyone could listen in on a call. Placing the call on a party line was deemed too big of a risk to take. The *Rhinelander Daily News* wrote that "the friend drove to Rhinelander because he had heard there is a direct wire from Chicago to Rhinelander, and he wished to use a telephone line that could not be tapped in some telephone exchange." Once he reached the safety of Rhinelander, a call was placed; after a transfer the message got through to Melvin Purvis, who headed the Chicago branch of the FBI.

Back at the lodge, Pat Reilly and Pat Cherrington departed for St. Paul where they were going to see underworld saloon owner Harry Sawyer, who had been holding some money for the gang. While Dillinger and the men were getting their future travel plans together, Melvin Purvis and the FBI were finalizing their own travel plans to Rhinelander (see Voss' Birchwood Lodge). Seemingly out of the blue, Dillinger announced a change of plans and decided that the gang would push up their departure time and take off as soon as Reilly and Cherrington returned from the Saintly City. Switching plans was nothing out of the ordinary for Dillinger, as he seemed to have an innate ability to sense when things were getting too dangerous. Perhaps the constant parade of visitors and family members caught the attention of his ever vigilant eye. Catching Dillinger had become Melvin Purvis' sole mission in life—it appeared that his whole career teetered on his ability to apprehend the elusive fugitive. With every second counting, Purvis and his men scrambled to reach Little Bohemia before Dillinger disappeared. Having chartered a plane, Purvis and his men flew into the Rhinelander airport, and after some difficulty they managed to secure some cars and took off toward Manitowish Waters. The night air was freezing and the snow-covered roads were mangled at best, making the ride through the woods a stressful operation. The caravan of cars pulled into Voss' Birchwood Resort to re-group (see Voss' Birchwood Resort).

At approximately 9pm the FBI approached Little Bohemia with their darkened cars. The night was black and the area was so wooded and mysterious that nearly anything seemed possible. Quickly the agents angled their cars across the lodge's only exit to the road. Although the agents were equipped with tear gas, machine guns, and bulletproof vests, the nervousness in the air was almost palpable. Most of the agents were relatively new to the force, and even more importantly, they were new to gunfights. Now as they were about to face off against the most hardened of criminals their minds swirled with doubt. It seemed like fate itself was against them when the Wanatka's dogs began barking furiously at the encroaching agents. However, the gangsters paid little attention to the dogs, which had been barking all weekend, and their alarm had lost its steam. Just moments after the dogs acted up, three local men started leaving the lodge after enjoying a few drinks with their Sunday dinner. Unaware of the danger that lurked from both inside and outside the building, the men casually walked out and started up their car. With their radio blaring, the trio looked to head home for the night. Not knowing the identities of the men, the FBI panicked and assumed that the gangsters had been alerted by the dogs, and were now making a run for it. Frantically the FBI demanded that the car halt, but the orders were drowned out by the booming radio. Not willing to let Dillinger escape, the agents opened fired and let loose a volley of lead on the car. All three men were struck by the bullets—one of them fatally. The *Manitowoc Herald Times* ran a statement from the U.S. Attorney General who explained that the event happened like this: "Before the house could be completely surrounded, three men left the house and got into an automobile. They were commanded to stop and were informed that the men ordering them to stop were government officers. They did not stop, and agents of the division shot at the tires of the automobile." With blood oozing from their wounds, the two surviving men fled from the car into the nearby woods. If the dogs did not awaken the attention of the gangsters, the FBI gunfire blasts certainly did. The *Iola Daily Register* wrote that "the shots warned Dillinger and his band, who had taken forcible possession of the resort Friday."

At this point in their criminal careers all of the gangsters were master escape artists, having had slipped by the authorities even in the most dire situations. As usual, Dillinger and his men remained eerily calm as they all headed for the back side of the building. Over the course of the previous days an elaborate escape plan had been de-vised and now it was sprung into action. For their part the FBI had been given an inaccurate map of the property layout which wrongly proposed that there was no possible way to escape from the rear of the lodge. In the complete darkness an agent spotted several shadows moving like ghosts near the back window. The agent quickly fired several rounds at the distant shapes and assumed he had forced whatever it was back inside. While the chaos was developing outside, Wanatka and the molls sought sanctuary in the building's basement. Baby Face was staying in one of the outside cabins nearby the lodge, and when the firestorm erupted he could have easily disappeared into the night without notice. However, true to his notorious reputation of loving a gunfight, Baby Face instead grabbed his gun and returned fire on the agents before retreating into the wilderness. The FBI, believing that they finally had the gangsters trapped, outmanned, and out gunned, lit up the night with gunfire. The onslaught of bullets tore through the entire lodge; windows shattered from the incoming lead, and those inside feared for their lives. The FBI had no idea that their worst nightmare had come true and that all of the gangsters were already well on their way to freedom.

Returning from St. Paul were Reilly and Cherrington, who upon seeing all of the commotion, wisely shut down their

 lights, slammed the car into reverse, and floored the pedal. After being fired on by the agents, the two would eventually make it out of the area and back to the safety of St. Paul. Dillinger, Hamilton, and Van Meter had slid down the embankment of the lodge and ran alongside the lake, covered from the sight of the FBI. The gang stumbled upon the residence of Mr. and Mrs. Mitchell, whose car had been

parked in their driveway. Desperate for a get-away vehicle, Dillinger and his men explained that they had no intentions of harming anyone, they simply needed the couple's car. Unfortunately, the Mitchells' vehicle wasn't in running shape, but another car in the driveway was and the owner, Robert Johnson, lived nearby. Van Meter and Hamilton ran over to his home and cleverly explained that Mrs. Mitchell was sick and needed a ride to the hospital. When Johnson came out he quickly discovered the ruse when an armed Van Meter was waiting for him. Johnson was forced to drive the gangsters out of town. Of all the gangsters, Tommy Carroll would have the easiest escape. After failing to keep up with the speed of the others, Carroll broke off on his own path. Carroll spotted a parked car, hotwired it, and sped off out of Wisconsin.

Back at the lodge things had simmered down a bit. The *Iola Daily Register* reported that "between midnight and dawn, the guns were silent. The federal agents then approached the house, forced open the door, and threw in tear gas bombs." The agents heard the voice of a man pleading that they all would come out as long as the FBI did not fire. Again the *Iola Daily Register* wrote that "three young women, between 20 and 25 years of age ran out, gasping and chocking." It is hard to imagine the elation that the Feds felt when they heard that the most wanted men in America were about to surrender to them. However, their dream was short-lived when the only ones to walk out were the lodge's staff and the gangster's molls. Although the realization of their blunder was instant, the ramifications would be eternal. Unimaginably deflated, the FBI hastily took inventory of the botched raid. Out of all the gangsters that were staying at the lodge, not a single one was apprehended or killed. In a publicity nightmare, it was revealed that of the three innocent victims shot at, two were injured and one was killed. Things got even worse when an escaping Baby Face shot up a car load of officers, severely injuring two of them, while killing the third. The fall-out from the debacle was immediate—newspapers around the country posted headlines of Dillinger's great escape and the FBI's big blunder.

Sensing the public outcry at the killing of innocent victims by the government hands, the FBI immediately began to

Three Girls Dillinger's Gang Left Behind

manipulate the media, and set into play a plethora of misinformation that would became its trademark for years to come. An *Associated Press* article in the *Sandusky Register* wrote, "John Dillinger, with hate in his heart and murder on his trigger finger, was believed somewhere in the wilderness of northern Wisconsin tonight." The *Sandusky Register* carried a much more sanitized version of events claiming that "about 10 p.m., three men, having regaled themselves with beer, walked out of Little Bohemia and stepped into their automobile. The waiting officers commanded them to halt. They failed to hear the order because their car radio was on. Watchdogs began barking. The machine gun on the roof let loose a deadly blast. The officers fired back and in the cross fire Boisoneau, one of the men who had stopped in for drinks, was killed." Even with the blatant reshaping of the facts, the FBI could not escape the public's disdain at their folly. Even humorist Will Rogers took a shot at the FBI telling newspapers, "Well, they had Dillinger surrounded and was all ready to shoot him when he come out, but another bunch of folks come out ahead, so they just shot them instead. Dillinger is going to accidentally get with some innocent bystanders some time, then he will get shot!" Melvin Purvis felt so personally responsible for the disaster at Little Bohemia that he sent his resignation to J. Edgar Hoover, who refused to accept it.

Wanatka's concerns that a gunfight with the Feds would ruin him financially proved to be entirely unfounded, as soon after news of the gun battle spread, the lodge was inundated with flocks of curious sight seekers. Today Little Bohemia continues to operate in the Northwoods, and although they no longer provide lodging, they have incredibly preserved the authentic feel of the 1930s in the restaurant and bar. Although it still remains a popular tourist destination, the workers always have time to share a gangster story or two. The place uses the advertising claim that "Dillinger only left because he had to," and after visiting Little Bohemia for yourself, you may feel the same way.

Tommy Gun Adventures:
While at Little Bohemia, make sure you check out the display of clothing, guns, and personal artifacts that the gangsters left behind. The lodge also continues to use the original windows that were shot up in the gunfight, and the bullet holes are still plainly visible.

Lac du Flambeau, WI

Baby Face Nelson
Spends the Night

THE WEATHER
Fair with freezing temperature 560 in cold in northwest portion tonight; Saturday warmer.

THE RHINELANDER DAILY NEWS

SEVENTEENTH YEAR—NO. 41   RHINELANDER, WIS., FRIDAY EVENING, APRIL 27, 1934

EIGHT PAGES TODAY
Two Looked Wire, SE
The Associated Press

PRICE FIVE CENTS

NELSON ESCAPES AT FLAMBEAU

Baby Face Spends the Night

Location:

Dillman's Bay Resort

Cabin #5 (Fisherman's Cabin)

3305 Sand Lake Lodge Lane

Lac du Flambeau, WI 54538

(715) 588-3143

www.dillmans.com

Directions:

From downtown Lac du Flambeau head north east on County Hwy D (Observation Tower Rd.). Turn left on Sand Lake Lodge Lane; follow it as it curves to the right and you will see the resort.

Gangster Lore:

The early 1900s must have been a spectacular time to experience the pristine nature of Wisconsin's Northwoods.

Today the area still holds plenty of wonder and excitement for the thousands of vacationing families seeking some solitude and relaxation among the beauty of the forests. But long before national restaurants and chain hotels started to litter the towns, the area enjoyed a more wild and carefree attitude that was matched only by the pioneer spirit of those who called the area home. Old timers recall the days when one pot-holed dirt road served as the main thoroughfare between towns. This was a time when the seclusion of the area seemed endless, bound only by one's imagination. Those who live here have fought hard to protect the treasured history and beauty of their area. Unfortunately, even the most vigilant preservation efforts cannot stop progress from slowly rearing its ugly head. Luckily, there are places that time seems to have forgotten, and Dillman's Bay Resort is one such place. In fact, the area is so amazing that Baby Face Nelson only left because he had to.

History:

1918 – Ben Gauthier purchased land on Sand Lake and opened the Ben Gauthier Resort.

1934 – Marvin Dillman and Peg Peterson learned that the Ben Gauthier Resort was up for sale. The couple purchased the resort with financing provided by Peg's father. The couple had the grand plan of transforming the resort into a boy's camp.

1934 – After the infamous shootout at Little Bohemia, Baby Face Nelson made his way to the cabin of Ollie Catfish, where he hid out for several days.

1935 – Soon after their purchase of the resort, Marvin and Peg were married on the grounds.

1930s – Looking to expand the resort, the couple purchased the old Catfish cabin and hauled it across the lake to the location where it sits today.

1939 – A fire broke out in an apartment on the backside of the hotel. A log from an unattended fire rolled out from the fire place and set the building ablaze. The main lodge was destroyed before help arrived and the fire was extinguished.

1940s-1990s – Over the years numerous changes occurred at the resort, including the passing of ownership down through several generations of the family.

1992 – Once again a fire broke out at the resort and consumed the main lodge.

1993 – In an effort to honor the history of the resort, a new lodge was constructed on the exact spot as the previous lodge.

2003 – Stephanie Robertson-Skotterud and her husband, Todd, took over the day-to-day operations of their family resort.

Currently – Dillman's Bay Resort is open to the public.

Investigation:

From the moment I stepped foot on the property, I felt like I was transported back to the heyday of Wisconsin's Northwoods. Filled with gorgeous cabins perched along White Sand Lake, Dillman's provides the perfect backdrop for anyone looking to get away from it all. Although Dillman's is a large and spacious resort, it has somehow managed to create a small welcoming feel. As I leisurely strolled the grounds, it was impossible not to feel the history of the place pouring out from all corners. Dillman's is so relaxing that I had to constantly remind myself that I wasn't there for a vacation, I was there to retrace the footsteps of one of America's most wanted criminals—George "Baby Face" Nelson.

Out of all the fugitives at Little Bohemia, Nelson had the most difficult time escaping the area (see Shootout at Little Bohemia). Baby Face had always been good with cars, but when both of the vehicles he was able to 'borrow' clunked out on him, Baby Face had no choice but to set off on foot through the pitch black forest. After walking all night through 18 miles of woods, a weary Nelson finally stumbled into the Lac du Flambeau Reservation. It was around noon when Nelson spotted a small-framed shack that was inhabited by Ollie (Ole) Catfish and his family. What happened next comes in several different versions. The *Manson City Globe-Gazette* wrote, "Nelson informed Catfish with unmistakable gestures he was going to have a guest for a few days." Ollie's own version of the story told to the *Associated Press* goes like this:

"I was in my cabin near town Monday afternoon with my wife and my kids and a friend. We were making maple syrup. Somebody knocked at door and when I go to see who was there, a man stepped inside. 'Take me to town,' he say. 'No,' I say. 'I make you go,' he said. 'I show you something.' Then he pulled a gun from his pocket and told me I should stop making syrup. Then he went over to the fire and put it out. I guess he didn't want folks to see smoke and come to my cabin."

Ollie's version of events was printed in numerous newspapers around the country. The media was hungry for any inside information about the dangerous fugitive, and Ollie delivered in spades. Yet, in their book *Baby Face Nelson*, authors Steven Nickel and William Helmer contend that when Nelson approached the cabin, he was greeted by Ollie's niece Mary. In fact, they claim that Ollie wasn't even home at the time when Nelson politely asked Mary if he could buy some lunch, as the smell from her baking awakened his appetite. After finishing off his meal, Nelson asked to lie down for a bit and explained that he had been walking for quite some time and was a little worn out. It was during Nelson's nap that Ollie finally made it home from town to discover their new dangerous guest. By then it was getting late and Nelson used the pending nightfall as an excuse to spend the evening with the family. Nelson informed his hosts he was a member of a hunting party who had somehow got turned around and now he was completely lost. Nelson was known to be a persuasive speaker, but here he faced an uphill battle because, like always, Nelson was dressed to the nines in a very expensive suit. His tailored clothing, along with his dress shoes, provided enough evidence for the Catfish family to cast doubt on his story. Once it was discovered that Nelson was in possession of three pistols, the family realized that he was on the run from the law.

Waiting for the 'heat' on him from Little Bohemia to die down, Nelson spent two more nights with the Catfish family. Even though Ollie told the *United Press* that Nelson "talked more like a baby than

Forced To Hide Dillinger Pal

Ollie Catfish and his wife (above). Indians living in the Lac du Flambeau district of northern Wisconsin, were unwilling hosts to George "Baby Face" Nelson, widely sought Dillinger gangster, for two days. Then Nelson forced Catfish to direct him out of the woods near the Indian's shack. (Associated Press Photo)

like man," it must have been a stressful time for the family. While Nelson was small in stature, his confidence and temper were more than enough to frighten the bravest of men. At this point in his crime career, Nelson was a master criminal who was adept at surviving and escaping from even the most difficult situations. Ollie commented on Nelson's vigilance in an interview with the *United Press* stating, "He didn't sleep. Watched me and woman and kids all time. He stayed right with me. Nobody could get away." Adding to the sense of being kidnapped, Ollie went on to state, "All time he just sat around. Didn't play with kids. He didn't shave. Cleaned his fingernails. All time he didn't sleep three days, three "nights". The *Huntingdon Daily News* reported, "For three days the gangster held Catfish and his family prisoners in their own home, refusing to allow anyone to go outside even to replenish the dwindling food supply."

Finally after three days of rural family life, Nelson began to get restless and expressed eagerness about leaving. At approximately 5pm, with the cover of darkness approaching, Nelson forced Ollie to guide him to town. The *Wisconsin State Journal* wrote that the two men "walked seven miles along the trail toward Flambeau." Once in town they encountered Adolph Goetz, a rural mail carrier and part time lawman, who happened to be fishing at Fence Lake. The *Laredo Times* reported that Nelson "pushed a gun into his ribs, and asked 'is that you car up on the hill?'" Goetz admitted that the vehicle was his, and perhaps sensing the seriousness of Nelson's character, quickly handed over his keys. Nelson was never afraid to throw around money, as evidenced when Ollie told the *Winnipeg Free Press* that once Nelson had the keys he "threw $20 in paper money on the ground to the man." Nelson then directed Ollie into their new found car and forced him to navigate the way to the junction of Highway 70. Once Nelson made it to Lac du Flambeau Road, Ollie was relieved of his hosting duties and dropped off on the side of the road. Ollie told the *Winnipeg Free Press* that Nelson threatened, "If you say anything about this, I'll kill you." With Ollie safely released, Nelson hightailed it out of the area as fast as he could. Relieved that no harm had come to himself, or his family, Ollie walked back into town where he notified the authorities of what had transpired over the last few days. Just a few moments earlier, Goetz had also alerted the authorities to the whereabouts of Baby Face, and even provided them with the license plate number of the stolen car.

The sensational news that Baby Face Nelson was still lingering in the area spread rapidly throughout the north. The *Sandusky Register* wrote, "Every woodsman who could be reached was called out with his deer rifle, shotgun, or pistol. All night posses searched the forests, routed families from bed in search of the elusive killer, and guarded highways and bridges." Although the organized search helped give the townsfolk some semblance of safety and control, their efforts were for naught, as Baby Face was already burning rubber towards the safety of Chicago.

While talking to the press and authorities, Ollie always maintained that Baby Face held his family hostage at gunpoint, and during the entire time he had never received a penny from the gangster. Regardless of how true this was, in a time when others were being prosecuted and sent to prison for harboring these gangsters, Ollie knew that it was better to play the victim. While no one really knows what truly happened during those three days, for someone who had garnered the reputation as a cold blooded manic, it is almost certain that when pressed, Baby Face would not have blinked at threatening innocent bystanders in order to get away. But Ollie's claim that he was not given a penny for his troubles seems a bit out of out of character for Nelson, who was widely known as a generous tipper and always made an effort to pay his own way. Nelson had an enormous chip on his shoulder and took great pride in always paying for things (except when he was robbing

ELUDES TRAP

nsom

DILLINGER GANG KILLER ELUDES POLICE TRAP

"Baby Face" Nelson Steals
Auto In Wisconsin Woods
And Escapes

GEORGE "BABY FACE"

banks). There are numerous stories of Nelson unwrapping a $10 bill from his money roll in order to pay for one or two dollars worth of food or gas, only to tell the clerk to keep the change. Authors Nickel and Helmer wrote that before Ollie was let out of the getaway car Nelson slipped him $75 to help offset his troubles. In his book, *Gangster Holidays*, Tom Hollatz includes a story from a local resident named Albert Cole, who remembered asking Catfish whether Baby Face had ever paid him for his troubles. Cole stated that Catfish was sticking to his original story of denial. Cole said, "But then I started to smile. He was wearing a new hat and some new shoes. We all knew…"

After some time, people began to forget about the great shootout of 1934, and slowly went about their business as usual. Out of financial necessity the Dillman family had scrapped the idea of turning the resort into a boy's camp, and soon found themselves trying to keep up with the growing demand for resort reservations. In an effort to expand their resort, they purchased the old Catfish family cabin that sat directly across the lake. With the lake thick with ice, the small cabin was hauled over to the resort, where it was coined the "Fisherman's Cabin." While giving me a tour, Todd told me that no one was sure as to the exact date when Ollie's cabin was brought over, but he guessed that it was in the 1930s or early 1940s. Over the years Ollie's old cabin has grown, adding another bedroom and expanding out with a Northwoods themed porch overlooking the tranquil lake. While the cabin has all the modern necessities it also maintains the original room where Baby Face spent the night back in 1934. I often write about the importance of keeping history alive, and whether good or bad, Dillman's Bay Resort provides you with one of the most unique opportunities available in Wisconsin—the chance to spend the night in the same place as Baby Face Nelson. But beware…Dillman's Bay Resort is a truly amazing resort. You may find yourself falling in love with the place, and much like Baby Face himself, you might only leave because you have to!

ALL OVER WISCONSIN

NEED MORE GANGSTERS

Need More Gangsters Hot Spots?

Wisconsin is overflowing with gangster history. The previous chapters were just the very start of legends that continue to circulate throughout the Badger State. If you haven't quite gotten your fill of gangsters yet, I have put together a few more places that will keep you traveling for a little while longer. Although these places are not quite as well-known as some of the others in the book, they certainly are just as appealing and interesting. Of course, be sure to ask around at these spots…you will be surprised at just how many other places you will discover.

Hayward

Herman's Landing LCO Resort
8255N Cty Rd CC
Hayward, WI 54843
(715) 462-3626

Gangster Lore:
Legend states that gangster Joey "The Doves" Aiuppa spent a lot of time in the Northwoods enjoying the wonderful outdoors. While out fishing one day Aiuppa latched onto a monster Muskie. After a fierce battle, the huge Muskie was finally landed. The gigantic fish weighed in at an amazing 69 pounds, 11 ounces—a new world record. The only problem was that Aiuppa was a syndicate boss in Chicago who happened to be on the lam from the law—a fact that made him unable to take credit for his catch. Legend states the Aiuppa

ended up selling the Muskie to well-known fisherman Louis Spray, who then registered the catch as his own, and claimed the glory that came from the world record. This legend has sparked a lot of discussion in the fishing world and is still hotly debated. Regardless of who actually caught the Muskie, Aiuppa wasn't the only mobster taking advantage of Hayward's great fishing, as numerous underworld characters kept the Hayward guides extremely busy for many years.

Hurley

Silver Street District
Entire Downtown – Hurley, WI
Hurley Area Chamber of Commerce
(715) 561-4334

Gangster Lore:
In its heyday Hurley was one wild and rambunctious destination. With the discovery of ore, the area ballooned in population overnight. Overflowing with lumberjacks, gamblers, miners, outlaws and speculators, the town had no shortage of unique characters. It was Hurley's widely known reputation as a sin city that attracted many of the vacationing gangsters, who spent a lot of time enjoying Hurley's secluded scenery along with its many saloons, gambling dens, and brothels. With so much illegal activity happening in this vice-ridden city, people started using the expression "Hurley or Hell," when describing the North-woods hot spot.

Mercer

In the 1930s, Al Capone's brother, Ralph Capone, purchased a luxurious cabin up north in the town of Mercer with his wife, Madeleine. While Ralph was nowhere near the criminal that Al was, he had his hand in plenty of illegal enterprises. In 1930, the *Chicago Tribune* listed Ralph as the number two public enemy in the country (Al was #1). Ralph was in charge of the bottling business and oversaw much of the gambling machine activity as well. In the 1940s, Ralph and Madeleine bought the Rex Hotel in downtown Mercer. Along with the hotel came the downstairs tavern called Billy's Bar. The building was said to have cost Capone $45,000. Legend states that Capone oversaw, and made quite of sum of money from, his interests in all of the slot machines that were spread through the bars of the Northwoods. In 1974, at the age of 81, Ralph Capone passed away after having suffered from poor health for many years. In true Northwoods fashion, whatever transgressions Ralph had committed in Chicago were forgotten by the people of Mercer, who described Ralph as a stand-up guy and one of the nicest neighbors you could ask for. Tales of Ralph's generosity were legendary in Mercer. If a family went without food, Ralph would step in and have groceries delivered to them. If a community cause was in need of manpower or financial assistance, Ralph was the first person to help. Even today you can find old timers in Mercer who remember Ralph as a kind, generous, and caring member of the community. The Rex Hotel is now the CITGO and Ralph's cabin is now privately owned.

Rex Hotel and Billy Bar –
Now CITGO Quick Food Mart
5206 N US Highway 51
Mercer, WI
(715) 476-2900

Ralph's Old Cabin – Now private residence
– Please view from road.
2073 W County Highway J
– "Wander" sign hanging in front yard.
Mercer, WI

Minocqua

Belle Isle Sports Bar and Grill
301 E Front St. Ste. 301
Minocqua, WI 54548
(715) 356-7444

Gangster Lore:

When the gangsters traveled to the Northwoods for some much needed rest and relaxation—gambling and drinking—they spent their evening testing their luck at the Belle Isle. The place actually opened up as "The Minocqua" and the upstairs of the establishment provided lodging for a variety of travelers. At one time the Minocqua even hosted famous guests, including the great showman P.T. Barnum, and U.S. President Benjamin Harrison. Over the years the place became a gangster hot spot, and while spending time up at Ma Bailey's House of Ill Repute, the outlaws would make Minocqua their vacation base because of its high energy nightlife. The Belle Isle enjoyed the reputation of being a hopping place where on any given night you could bump into some of the country's most wanted men. The place was packed full of slot machines, card games, and other games of "chance." Of course, during Prohibition the place also had a steady supply of liquor to keep the clientele happy and spending. The old Belle Isle is still in operation today, and you can pop in for a quick drink…just be sure to tell them Ma Bailey sent you.

Norwood Pines Supper Club
10171 Hwy 70 W
Minocqua, WI 54548
(715) 356-3666

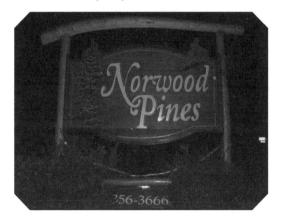

Gangster Lore:
With all the well-to-do gangsters roaming the Northwoods, it seems only fitting that the area provided them with several high-end dining options. One the gangsters' favorite places was the elegant Norwood Pines, which played host to the vacationing men and their molls. The same architect

that designed Little Bohemia also did the designs for the Norwood. Built in 1937, the restaurant would have missed out on the early gangsters like Capone and Dillinger, but still saw their fair share of outlaws. Legend states that the upstairs of the restaurant was used as a brothel. Guests from Chicago would fly in for the weekend before heading back to their daily lives in the Windy City. Grisly tales tell of a gangster and his mistress being gunned down by a rival while staying inside the Norwood. Even after all these years, the Norwood Pines is still serving both residents and visitors meals fit for a gangster.

Miscauno Island

Four Seasons Resort
N16800 Shoreline Drive
Pembine, WI 54156
(715) 324-5244 or (877) 324-5244
www.fourseasonswi.com

Gangster Lore:
The upscale Miscauno resort opened for business in 1905. Expense was no concern for the builders of the resort which came complete with a massive fireplace, modern amenities, and Tiffany Chandeliers. Fire ravaged through the building in 1923, leaving only the fireplace intact. Two short years later the resort was rebuilt around the original fireplace and was named the Four Seasons Club. Although the resort attracted celebrities, elected officials, and some of the na-

tion's most wealthy, it was one guest that overshadowed all of the others…Al Capone. It is said that Capone frequently visited the resort with dozens of his colleagues as they took in the fresh Wisconsin air. For years, stories of Capone's alleged visits have entertained both the staff and guests. Whether or not Capone used the resort as a vacation destination only adds to the charm of this 100-year-old treasure.

<u>Rhinelander</u>

Bugsy's Brown Street Brewery
16 North Brown Street
Rhinelander, WI 54501-3160
(715) 369-2100

Gangster Lore:
The old saloon dates back to the days before Prohibition. The building itself had a spider web of underground tunnels leading to various locations throughout town. It is alleged

that these tunnels provided the perfect venue for illegal booze to be smuggled into the tavern. Of course the tunnels also made for a nice escape route for those looking for a quick getaway from the authorities. It is thought that the saloon was also a favorite watering hole for "Scarface" Al Capone. During his numerous trips through Wisconsin, Capone was said to stop in for a couple drinks at the saloon. The bar is still open under the ironic name Bugsy's Brown Street Brewery, since Bugs Moran was one of Capone's fiercest enemies.

Minnesota Road Guide
to Gangster Hotspots

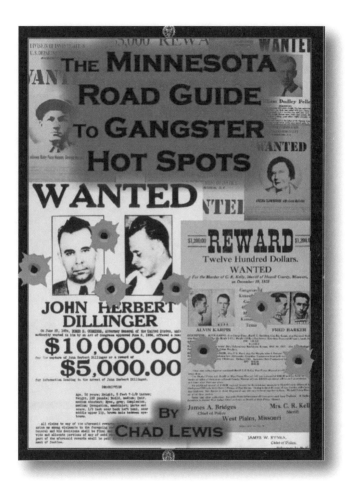

Get your gangster fill at

www.ontheroadpublications.com

Bio

Chad Lewis –Is a researcher, author, and lecturer, on topics of the strange and unusual. He has a Master of Science Degree in Psychology and has traveled the globe in search of unique and bizarre stories and history. Chad's research has been featured on numerous national TV shows, radio interviews, magazines, and newspaper articles. Chad is the co-author of the Haunted Road Guide series and the author of the Hidden Headlines series.

You can reach Chad at chadlewis44@hotmail.com